SUSTAINABLE TOURISM AFTER COVID-19

INSIGHTS AND RECOMMENDATIONS FOR ASIA AND THE PACIFIC

DECEMBER 2021

ASIAN DEVELOPMENT BANK

ADB

Contents

Tables, Figures, and Boxes

Boxes

Foreword

The coronavirus disease (COVID-19) pandemic has wrought unprecedented devastation on tourism in Asia and the Pacific. Tourism arrivals fell by 84% in 2020 compared to 2019, making it the worst affected region in the world. Countries heavily dependent on tourism also experienced the largest fall in economic output. This abrupt drop demonstrated the importance of tourism for the region, but also placed a spotlight on its negative impacts. Decreased economic activity—including tourism—resulted in the largest annual reduction in CO_2 emissions in more than 70 years, for example. Furthermore, natural sites suffering from overtourism prior to the pandemic started to recover.

As a result of this historic shock, host communities, national governments, and tourism operators have started to engage in discussions on how to rebuild the sector to make it more resilient to shocks and with greater respect for ecological boundaries. At the same time, tourists themselves have developed a new appreciation for the importance of ensuring that tourism is sustainable and beneficial for all stakeholders. Consequently, there is now a unique window of opportunity to reflect on the lessons learned in the last 2 years and put in place reforms that enable tourism to contribute to more green, resilient, inclusive, and sustainable development pathways.

It has become clear that the road to tourism recovery will be longer and with greater twists and turns than imagined at the beginning of the pandemic. New variants of COVID-19 and challenges in accessing and administering vaccinations mean national governments and tourism operators are dealing with multiple cycles of opening and locking down. A full recovery of the tourism sector to prepandemic levels is not expected any time soon.

The difficult recovery from the pandemic is compounded by another problem. Countries in Asia and the Pacific must contend with the worsening impacts of the climate crisis. Consequently, it is critical that assistance measures and policies, which seek to reduce the economic impact of the pandemic, also create incentives and opportunities for a positive transformation in tourism. For example, employment support programs can be linked to the training of tourism workers to improve their digital technology skills or their capacity to deal with disaster situations. The region should not seek to "build *back* better" but rather to "build *forward* better."

Looking ahead, national governments need to create an enabling environment for tourism industries that focuses on quality rather than quantity. This can be achieved by building governance structures that allow for genuine partnerships with host communities. They can also encourage sustainable businesses with incubator schemes or certification programs.

It is also important that tourism destinations improve their resilience by diversifying their tourism markets. In many places in Asia and the Pacific, this will mean marketing and developing products for domestic tourism. It also means that investments in tourism infrastructure such as hotels and conference centers should be designed to be multipurpose and adaptable to changing requirements.

To finance a positive transformation of tourism, new revenue sources will be needed. Levying bed taxes or entry costs to individual attractions can help raise revenues locally. At the national level, green bonds for tourism provide a growing opportunity. Risk sharing mechanisms can also help by encouraging private investment in sustainable tourism projects.

This report examines trends, dynamics, vulnerabilities, and opportunities associated with tourism development and how the sector has been impacted by COVID-19. It offers concrete recommendations to policymakers and industry stakeholders in developing member countries (DMCs) of the Asian Development Bank (ADB). These recommendations look at how governments can initiate the recovery of tourism industries and how to leverage tourism to foster sustainable development in Asia and the Pacific. ADB has a long history of support—both direct and indirect—to tourism industries in its DMCs. The bank supports the financing of critical infrastructure, investments in tourism enterprises, and regional collaboration on cross-border tourism. In this very challenging and transformative time for the tourism industry, ADB stands ready to support its DMCs to provide financial help as well as technical knowledge to transform this crisis into an opportunity.

Bambang Susantono
Vice-President for Knowledge Management and Sustainable Development
Asian Development Bank

Acknowledgments

This publication was jointly produced two teams at the Asian Development Bank (ADB): the Regional Cooperation and Integration Division (ERCI) of the Economic Research and Regional Department (ERCD) and the Regional Cooperation and Integration Thematic Group (RCI-TG) of the Sustainable Development and Climate Change Department (SDCC). It was supported by ADB under the Knowledge and Support Technical Assistance (TA) project 6628: Promoting Innovations in Regional Cooperation and Integration in the Aftermath of COVID-19. This TA support included financing from the Asia Regional Trade and Connectivity Fund established by the United Kingdom (UK) under the Regional Cooperation and Integration Financing Partnership Facility.

Anna Fink, Economist (Regional Cooperation), SDCC, and Matthias Helble, Senior Economist (ERCI), jointly led the effort to coordinate and contribute to the development and production of the publication. Ronald Butiong, Chief of Regional Cooperation and Integration Thematic Group, and Cyn-Young Park, Director, ERCI provided overall guidance and support.

Susanne Becken and Johanna Loehr of Griffith University, Australia led the drafting of the report including research, analysis, and stakeholder consultations. Sanya Grover provided research assistance. Apisalome Movono, Jutamas Wisansing, and Elaine Chiao Ling Yang contributed specific sections and added rich analyses to the report.

Stakeholder consultations have been of significant value, and the authors thank all of the experts interviewed. This publication also benefited from the valuable guidance and advice of colleagues in ADB working on the tourism sector, specifically Erik Aelbers, Dominic Mellor, Masato Nakane, Carmen Maria Garcia Perez, and Steve Schipani. Sandra Carvao and Zoritsa Urosevic of the United Nations World Tourism Organization also provided important reflections and considerations that have helped to shape the work.

A team of ADB consultants supported the production of this publication comprising Roble Poe Velasco-Rosenheim as editor, Melanie Kelleher as copy editor, Cherry Lynn Zafaralla as proofreader, Lumina Datamatics for typesetting and layout, and Mike Cortes for the graphic design of the cover. Wilhelmina Paz, Senior Economics Officer, and Melanie Pre, Operations Analyst, SDCC, provided valuable administrative support. The publishing team of ADB's Department of Communications provided support for the production and finalization of this publication.

Abbreviations

ADB	Asian Development Bank
ASEAN	Association of Southeast Asian Nations
CO_2	carbon dioxide
COVID-19	coronavirus disease
ERCI	Regional Cooperation and Integration Division
GDP	gross domestic product
GSTC	Global Sustainable Tourism Council
MSMEs	micro, small, and medium-sized enterprises
MST	Measuring Sustainable Tourism initiative
MTCO	Mekong Tourism Coordinating Office
OECD	Organisation for Economic Co-operation and Development
SDCC	Sustainable Development and Climate Change Department
SDG	Sustainable Development Goal
SPTO	South Pacific Tourism Organization
TSA	Tourism Satellite Account
UNWTO	United Nations World Tourism Organization
VICE	visitors, industry, community, and the environment
WEF	World Economic Forum

Executive Summary

This report explores the contributions of the tourism sector to achieving the Sustainable Development Goals (SDGs) before, during, and after the coronavirus disease (COVID-19) pandemic. It provides concrete recommendations on how policymakers and industry stakeholders can leverage tourism to foster sustainable development in Asia and the Pacific. This executive summary highlights key takeaways and recommendations from the report.

Chapter 1: Introduction

Tourism has become a key driver of socioeconomic growth in Asia and the Pacific. It employs roughly 150 million people in the region and provides opportunities to strengthen communities and ecosystems. However, in the absence of robust governance and planning, tourism growth threatens to overburden communities and ecosystems, while overlooking opportunities to foster inclusive and sustainable development.

The COVID-19 pandemic has disrupted virtually all aspects of tourism, reducing international travel by 74% in 2020 and producing cascading effects on businesses, governments, and communities alike. Despite its many challenges, the pandemic presents a unique opportunity for tourism stakeholders to step back and evaluate the sector and how it can contribute more effectively to sustainable development. Tourism is often misunderstood, as it involves a complex web of stakeholders, economic sectors, destinations, and communities. It is therefore important, at the outset, to establish a shared framework for analyzing tourism and its linkages to the Sustainable Development Goals (SDGs). Sustainable tourism is not a particular kind of travel—it is not only eco-tourism or tourism that is self-sustaining—rather, all types of tourism can also become sustainable if they help achieve the SDGs, revive the environment, or help communities thrive.

Chapter 2: Pre-COVID-19 Tourism and Sustainable Development in Asia and the Pacific

Tourism has many dimensions, and these can be analyzed through the lenses of visitors, industry, communities, and the environment or collectively, the VICE model. Sustainable tourism considerations related to the VICE model include the following:

Visitors. Before the pandemic, many countries focused on international tourists. However, Asian markets often receive more domestic visitors than international ones, and this dynamic can increase resilience to external shocks. Despite the importance of local tourism, many countries know little about their domestic markets. In addition to origin, a reason for visitor travel is often correlated to how much they spend. Business and wellness tourism are two examples of high-yield segments gaining traction in the region. There is also a growing focus on attracting visitors that contribute to target markets like organic food or community-based tourism. Tools like behavior pledges and carbon offset programs can encourage responsible visitor behavior.

Industry. Although most tourism businesses (by volume) are small and medium-sized enterprises, large businesses contribute more capital and as a result, often have more influence on how tourism develops. The voices of small enterprises should be heard and the distribution of benefits to different types of businesses, subsectors, and communities understood. Labor market issues impact the sustainability of tourism including, skills pools, inequality between women and men in accessing jobs and decision-making roles, and labor rights for informal workers.

Community and Culture. If managed effectively, tourism can help revive cultures, languages, customs, and traditions. Positive trends include support for local economic integration and destination stewardship driven by the local community. Conversely, increased tourism can lead to land-grab as destinations gain popularity, which can undermine social fabrics and create negative sentiments toward tourists. Good governance and community involvement in tourism planning are essential for managing perceptions and ensuring tourism genuinely supports a community to thrive.

Environment. The "environment" dimension considers how tourism interacts with climate change, resource management, and ecosystems. Climate considerations involve both impacts on destinations (such as the effects of hurricanes on coastal towns); and conversely, how tourism contributes to emissions, including through transportation to the destination. Resource management is critical to the sustainability of tourism. For instance, plastic pollution undermines tourism sustainability, while efficient energy or water use can improve tourism performance. Biodiversity and tourism can have both positive and negative impacts. Positive ones are linked to travelers protecting specific ecosystems—like the Great Barrier Reef—but these are often counterbalanced by increased emissions from travel, which ultimately harm the destination.

Enabling factors. Five thematic areas have proven instrumental in supporting the contribution of tourism to achieving the SDGs:

(i) **Governance.** Historically, the private sector has guided tourism governance; however, deeper public sector involvement may support growth in line with the SDGs.
(ii) **Policy.** Policies have traditionally focused on economic aspects of tourism, such as providing goods and service tax deductions. More can be done to encourage stewardship and collaboration while restricting harmful practices.
(iii) **Infrastructure and technology.** Investing in both hard infrastructure (like roads and airports) and digital infrastructure is a major pathway for governments to support tourism. Increasingly, border crossing software can streamline travel and build security.
(iv) **Research and data.** High-quality data is essential for making sound decisions. However, since tourism is cross disciplinary, there is limited large-scale research, and existing materials focus on economics as opposed to sustainability.
(v) **Education and training.** There are persistent skills shortages affecting tourism businesses in Asia and the Pacific. There is a need for more training programs, and to integrate sustainability considerations into hospitality and similar curricula.

Chapter 3: COVID-19 Impacts and Responses in Asia and the Pacific

In April 2020, 90% of the world had implemented full or partial travel restrictions, leading to the steepest drop in arrivals ever recorded—a decline of 1 billion international arrivals from 2019 to 2020. Asia had more severe impacts, with an 84% decline in international arrivals compared to 74% worldwide. Decreased tourism and economic activity have had some positive impacts on the environment, including the largest annual reduction in carbon dioxide (CO_2) emissions (7%) since World War II (Le Quéré et al. 2020). However, long-term environmental impacts will depend on how "green" recovery is, and whether support packages address environmental challenges. Although prospects for recovery vary widely by subsector, destination, and market segment, overall economic damages have been substantial:

(i)   **Accommodation industry.** In December 2020, most accommodation properties had reopened, but occupancy rates remained low and revenue per room had dropped by 59% across all open hotels in Asia (excluding the People's Republic of China), and by 47% in Australia and Oceania.

(ii) **Airports and cruises.** In 2020, airports lost $111.8 billion in revenue against business-as-usual, airlines lost $371 billion, and the cruise industry lost 99.5% of its revenue (ICAO 2021).

(iii) **Arts and culture.** Early in the pandemic, 90% of countries closed World Heritage sites and about 85,000 museums. Revenue losses may lead to site closure or deterioration.

(iv) **Jobs.** A study by the International Labour Organization on tourism workers in 14 countries in Asia and the Pacific found that 15.3 million workers were at risk of losing their jobs due to COVID-19, with millions more at risk in countries not surveyed.

Business responses have varied by subsector and destination, but have included reduced staff and services, temporary shutdowns, cost reductions, product adaptation, maintenance and training, digitization of operations, and sharing staff with businesses in higher demand.

At the policy level, governments have implemented three main types of response:

(i)   business support programs including loans, or nationalization of strategically important firms, like airlines;

(ii) sectoral schemes, training and capacity building programs, or workforce support programs; and

(iii) untargeted support providing liquidity to firms, and job-retention schemes.

Policy measures are designed for different time horizons—including making it through the crisis—adapting to the new normal, and cultivating resilience. The latter may provide the most opportunities for embedding sustainability into the future development of tourism. However, few policies have taken a long-term focus, such as including sustainability criteria in financial support packages, extending social protection, or helping redesign tourism systems.

Chapter 4: Expert Insights

This chapter provides expert insights into three areas that deserve close attention. It looks at the impact of COVID-19 on women working in tourism, which is important for ensuring social inclusion as tourism recovers. It also looks at the impact of the pandemic on Pacific island countries and Thailand, which hold important lessons on how to approach the transformation of tourism.

Elaine Chiao Ling Yang, Griffith University on Women in Tourism

Women in tourism are disproportionately affected by pandemic-induced unemployment, due to gender segregation and because they are overrepresented in casual and front-facing jobs. Migrant female workers—especially undocumented migrants and those in the informal sector (including sex workers)—are susceptible to precarious employment and exploitation in normal times, which is compounded during crises. The transition from crisis to recovery planning offers opportunities to embed gender equality into recovery through the following:

(i)   **Collecting gender-disaggregated data.** Gender-disaggregated data on secondary impacts (economic, social, and health) should inform inclusive recovery policies.

(ii) **Mainstreaming gender.** Response and recovery plans should feature gender and include women in their design and implementation. It is also necessary to address the vulnerability of female migrant workers to exploitation and violence.

(iii) **Upskilling and reskilling women.** Halts in tourism present opportunities for governments and tourism businesses to invest in capacity building. Upskilling female tourism workers can address the concentration of women in lower level jobs.

Apisalome Movono, Massey University, on Pandemic Impacts in the Pacific Islands

Tourism-dependent communities in the Pacific suffered significant financial difficulties due to the loss of tourism-based income: 73% of those completing a survey in mid-2020 said they had experienced a "major decline" in household income, and 60% of respondents were from households that relied on tourism for half of household total revenue (Scheyvens and Movono 2020). However, responses have highlighted Pacific resilience and sustainable pathways forward:

(i) **Returning to tradition.** People from the Pacific are relearning and reinvigorating indigenous knowledge and diversifying their skill sets. Traditional governance structures and resource sharing have supported communities suffering declines in tourism.

(ii) **Rebuilding the sector.** Recognizing opportunities to drive sector-wide reform, tourism workers are urging governments to promote off-season tourism, open new destinations to avoid crowding, and spread benefits more widely. Pacific governments are also exploring ways to attract high-value visitors and leverage tourism to achieve the SDGs.

(iii) **Resilience and regionalism.** A long-term approach may be critical to building tourism resilience to the pandemic and future threats. Regional organizations and national governments are exploring ways to collaborate on increasing sector resilience.

Jutamas Wisansing, Perfect Link Consulting Group on the Thai Tourism Transformation

Tourism has played a major role in the economic growth of Thailand, with a 485% increase in tourist arrivals from 1997 to 2019. However, growth and development have been concentrated in relatively few destinations within the country, and benefits have not been distributed evenly. Critics have long questioned whether tourism growth has improved the quality of life for Thai people. As the country rebuilds its tourism industry, the shift from response to sustainable recovery should involve a transformational change in mindsets; that a good place to live will always be a good place to visit, and not the other way around. Tourism in Thailand is doing the following to achieve this:

(i) **Targeting dispersal and domestic travel.** The pandemic highlights the need to rebalance demand for destinations nationally, and to encourage Thai people to travel.

(ii) **Rebranding.** Thai tourism is often associated with budget travel. While still a topic of debate, many believe it should target high-value visitors and emphasize sustainability.

(iii) **Aligning tourism with national strengths and development goals.** Thailand is shifting its development goals to support greener and more inclusive growth, and policymakers are encouraged to leverage tourism to achieve these objectives.

Chapter 5: Future Pathways and Opportunities

Future scenarios envisioned by the Forum for the Future (2020) provide a framework for identifying risks and opportunities for future tourism trajectories after the pandemic.

Discipline—The Age of Technology

Under this possible trajectory, technology helps increase government control over visitors and businesses. Examples include vaccine passport programs and enhanced data collection. This trajectory foresees improved efficiency through automation and the digitization of businesses operations and may allow emissions reductions.

Risks		Opportunities	
(i)	Loss of consumer privacy and increased power of government and large businesses	(i)	Technology improvements support better waste, water, and energy efficiency
(ii)	Exclusion or disadvantaging of some countries, businesses, or travelers	(ii)	Improved coordination regionally to standardize travel and health requirements
(iii)	High investment needs in digital infrastructure may overshadow other investment needs	(iii)	Increased government controls and the digitization of travel reduce emissions
(iv)	Increased standardization threatens diversity	(iv)	Greater data collection can improve decision-making and product development

Compete and Retreat—The End of Globalization

This trajectory pictures a future of nationalism or regionalism, and a decline in global solidarity. Tourism becomes mostly domestic, and countries prioritize self-sufficiency. Many countries took a national approach during the pandemic, for example by closing borders, prioritizing national citizens over migrant workers, supporting national firms, and vaccinating their people first. Varying access to resources and tourism markets may drive inequality under this trajectory.

Risks		Opportunities	
(i)	Growing inequality between countries	(i)	Increased localism and community resilience
(ii)	Decreased efficiency and sustainability as countries revert to siloed national solutions	(ii)	Revival of cultural practices and local identity
(iii)	Competing approaches and standards to sustainability, diverging between countries	(iii)	Local supply chains reduce leakage and are buffered against external disruptions
(iv)	Limited exchange of information	(iv)	Reduced aviation decreases emissions

Unsettled—Crisis as the New Normal

This future imagines a world moving from one shock to another, including resource scarcity, climate events, and extended conflict. People will be less inclined to engage in tourism as they deal with immediate problems over leisure. Under this scenario, broad progress against the SDGs will be difficult to achieve, and the adaptability of businesses and governments will be of primary importance. This scenario calls for transforming business models, strengthening governance, and diversifying markets to build the resilience of tourism.

Risks		Opportunities	
(i)	Mounting damages force actors into response mode over proactive planning	(i)	New products focusing on health, wellness, and nature may be in higher demand
(ii)	High costs of managing multiple crises	(ii)	Destinations with nearby markets may experience more tourism as visitors continue to travel, but closer to home
(iii)	Travel systems will be restructured, and traveler confidence may be low		
(iv)	Vulnerable groups will experience disproportional burdens	(iii)	Resource scarcity may encourage greater efficiency in production and consumption

Transform—A Shift in Mindset

This trajectory envisions a more sustainable, equitable, and low-carbon world. It requires the largest shift in mindsets and economic systems. This scenario pictures tourism industries that provide more equitable employment opportunities, support travel and accommodation options that waste and emit less, and encourage greater stewardship of communities and ecosystems. Finance and funding for environmentally friendly infrastructure will be critical, as will deeper coordination between the public and private sectors. The pathway requires a combination of incentivizing sustainable behavior alongside regulations to discourage unsustainable behavior.

Risks		Opportunities	
(i)	Countries have different levels of readiness to achieve sustainable growth and to decarbonize	(i)	A focus on thriving and well-being may address other issues, like those related to physical and mental health
(ii)	The transition needs to be managed so that the vulnerable are not disadvantaged or left behind	(ii)	Rapid action on climate change will help reduce the risk of climate disasters and prevent loss of life and capital
(iii)	There may be opposition to change	(iii)	Increased community cohesion will lead to healthy and resilient destinations
(iv)	Those who do not adapt to new business models or regulations may go out of business	(iv)	People reconnecting to nature encourages a revival of ecosystems
		(v)	Increased demand for nature tourism and sustainable experiences enhance business practices and products.

Chapter 6: Recommendations for Decision-Makers

The term "build back better" is often used when describing the recovery of tourism. The region, however, should not seek to recapture the tourism of the prepandemic era but rather "build *forward* better". This means creating a new kind of tourism that is more closely aligned to the Sustainable Development Goals.

Transforming tourism so that it genuinely contributes to achieving the SDGs will require a mix of incentives and disincentives, targeting action across the public and private sectors. Among the most pressing barriers to sustainable tourism in the region is the lack of good governance structures to support long-term planning, collaboration, and management. There is also a pressing need to include the voices of marginalized groups in sector development, including communities, the informal economy, and small businesses. While the recommendations are primarily for policymakers, they address topics that will also be of interest to commercial stakeholders and development partners. The report provides six pathways for encouraging the sustainable development of tourism, each with subsequent recommendations.

Value-Driven Tourism

(i)   Focus on quality and yield by attracting visitors that spend more and who wish to engage genuinely with the communities and destinations they visit.
(ii)   Ensure tourism activities are aligned with the carrying capacity of destinations and communities by understanding socioecological limits and leveraging planning, enforcement, and technology to manage tourism accordingly.
(iii)   Leverage uniqueness of place through appropriate at-place design of infrastructure and experiences, and by developing place-sensitive destination management strategies.
(iv)   Measure and report on progress in a transparent manner.

Decarbonizing Tourism

(i)   Design and implement decarbonization pathways that include clear targets and leverage economic instruments (like carbon markets) to encourage and track action.
(ii)   Take a collaborative approach to develop sustainable aviation fuels.
(iii)   Raise awareness and build carbon literacy through education, training, and certification and labeling schemes that can be aligned with visitor pledges.
(iv)   Support low-carbon industry practices by rewarding low-carbon behavior and designing minimum regulatory requirements to limit high-polluting activities.

Tourism-Led Regeneration

(i)   Foster ecological restoration by encouraging industry and visitors to contribute, and by integrating sustainability and restoration activities into licenses and concessions.

(ii)   Protect communities and encourage cultural thriving by
    (a)   ensuring they have a voice in tourism planning,
    (b)   developing rules or standards on how to tourism interacts with communities, and
    (c)   supporting mentorship and community networks.
(iii)   Ensure tourism is inclusive and supportive of health and subjective well-being by designing experiences that connect people with nature, and by implementing proactive risk management and health and safety standards.
(iv)   Empower local communities and small businesses by providing training to support entrepreneurs, and by encouraging businesses of all sizes to participate in tourism.

Diversification

(i)   Diversify tourism markets—including those for domestic visitors—by revising marketing campaigns and potentially discouraging unsustainable markets.
(ii)   Diversify products and encourage ones that support giving back, engaging local stakeholders, and localizing supply chains to reduce economic leakage.
(iii) Support workforce diversity and cultivate wider skill sets by providing training in soft skills and transferrable skills.
(iv)   Foster economic diversification by encouraging the integration of tourism into other sectors, and by removing policies that may not favor tourism.

Improving Tourism Governance

(i)   Integrate tourism policy considerations across sectors by building an understanding of tourism in non-tourism government departments, and by encouraging cross-sector collaboration in government and industry.
(ii)   Foster cooperation and public–private partnerships by leveraging framework agreements to encouraging data sharing and joint monitoring and evaluation; and by supporting local stakeholder networks (comprising public and private actors) to engage in planning and implementation.
(iii) Invest in strategy, ethical marketing, technology, and human capacity to drive a transformation in tourism markets and encourage more sustainable behavior.
(iv)   Build capacity in disaster risk management and adaptation by
    (a)   training people to manage and respond to disasters,
    (b)   investing in early warning systems, and
    (c)   creating strategic links between the tourism and humanitarian sectors.

Aligning Tourism Finance with Sustainability

(i)   Seek new revenue sources that can be reinvested into sustainable management of tourism. This can be nationally applied by local government—such as a bed tax—or applied by individual attractions, such as entry costs to a national park. Voluntary contributions through fundraising events can complement mandatory pricing mechanisms.
(ii)   Enable smaller-scale green finance to support tourism development by
    (a)   tailoring options to be more accessible to smaller firms,
    (b)   encouraging crowdfunding and microdonations, and
    (c)   developing risk-sharing mechanisms to increase access to finance for businesses of varying sizes.
(iii) Include sustainability criteria in assessing tourism projects and ensure that green finance evaluation criteria include sustainability considerations.
(iv)   Integrate sustainable tourism considerations into other sectors, such as transport or urban infrastructure projects, to maximize the value of projects across sectors.

1   Introduction

Rationale for the Report

Tourism has become one of the most important export earners for countries in Asia and the Pacific. It generates jobs and provides livelihoods to those in remote areas and can contribute to environmental protection by using revenue to support preservation. At the same time, sector growth often creates external costs for communities and the environment, and economic benefits are not always distributed equitably. The question of how to maximize benefits while minimizing pressures is central to decision-makers in the field.

The coronavirus disease (COVID-19) has put a halt to many forms of tourism, creating major impacts on associated industries and communities. However, this pause presents a window to reflect on the prepandemic tourism system, its trends, vulnerabilities, and opportunities. This window provides opportunities to "reset" tourism and to ensure it generates better sustainable development outcomes (United Nations 2020). This report describes the impacts of COVID-19 on tourism and seeks to assess the potential of the sector to contribute to the Sustainable Development Goals (SDGs) in Asia and the Pacific.

This chapter establishes a framework for interpreting tourism in the context of the SDGs, recognizing multiple facets of the tourism industry, including destinations and their socioecological systems, marketing, policy and investments, regional cooperation, and global frameworks. Chapter 2 provides a synopsis of how tourism can be sustainable, while Chapter 3 describes the impacts of COVID-19 on tourism in the region and immediate responses to the crisis. Chapter 4 provides three in-depth assessments of gender and select markets, and Chapter 5 explores future pathways for tourism. Chapter 6 makes policy recommendations for "building forward better." The report is intended for policymakers engaged in tourism and related sectors, and will also support organizations involved in overseas investment, development, and cooperation.

Defining a Framework for Sustainable Tourism

Tourism involves experiences away from home. Despite drastic changes in the industry, the core motives of travelers have remained much the same. These include the desire to escape, explore, and relax; and to achieve prestige, deeper relationships, and education. However, COVID-19 may have changed the priorities of tourists.

Tourism is often not well understood since it impacts many different economic sectors, people, and locations. It is therefore important—at the outset—to define sustainable tourism and a framework for analysis. Sustainable tourism is not only ecotourism or tourism that is self-sustaining. Richard Sharpley—when reflecting on 20 years of progress in sustainable tourism—argues that the concept of sustainable tourism is often a form of "greenwashing" and that international investment has often focused more on the growth of tourism (jobs and income) than on how tourism can be used to increase well-being. With the onset of COVID-19, however, the notion that sustainable tourism can enable transformations in the industry has gained momentum. Sustainable tourism is therefore tourism that helps to achieve the SDGs, revives the environment, or enables tourists and host communities to thrive.

Sustainable tourism is not a special form of travel, but all forms of tourism can become sustainable and support development. Achieving this requires a focus on the needs of local communities and the environment. In the broadest sense, tourism can contribute to all SDGs if it receives support from a range of international stakeholders (Figure 1). Research by the United Nations (UNWTO and UNEP 2017) suggests that tourism is most equipped to support three specific goals—SDG8 (Decent Work and Economic Growth), SDG12 (Responsible Consumption and Production), and SDG17 (Partnerships). This report highlights the links between tourism and the SDGs and provides recommendations on how to maximize complementarities in the future.

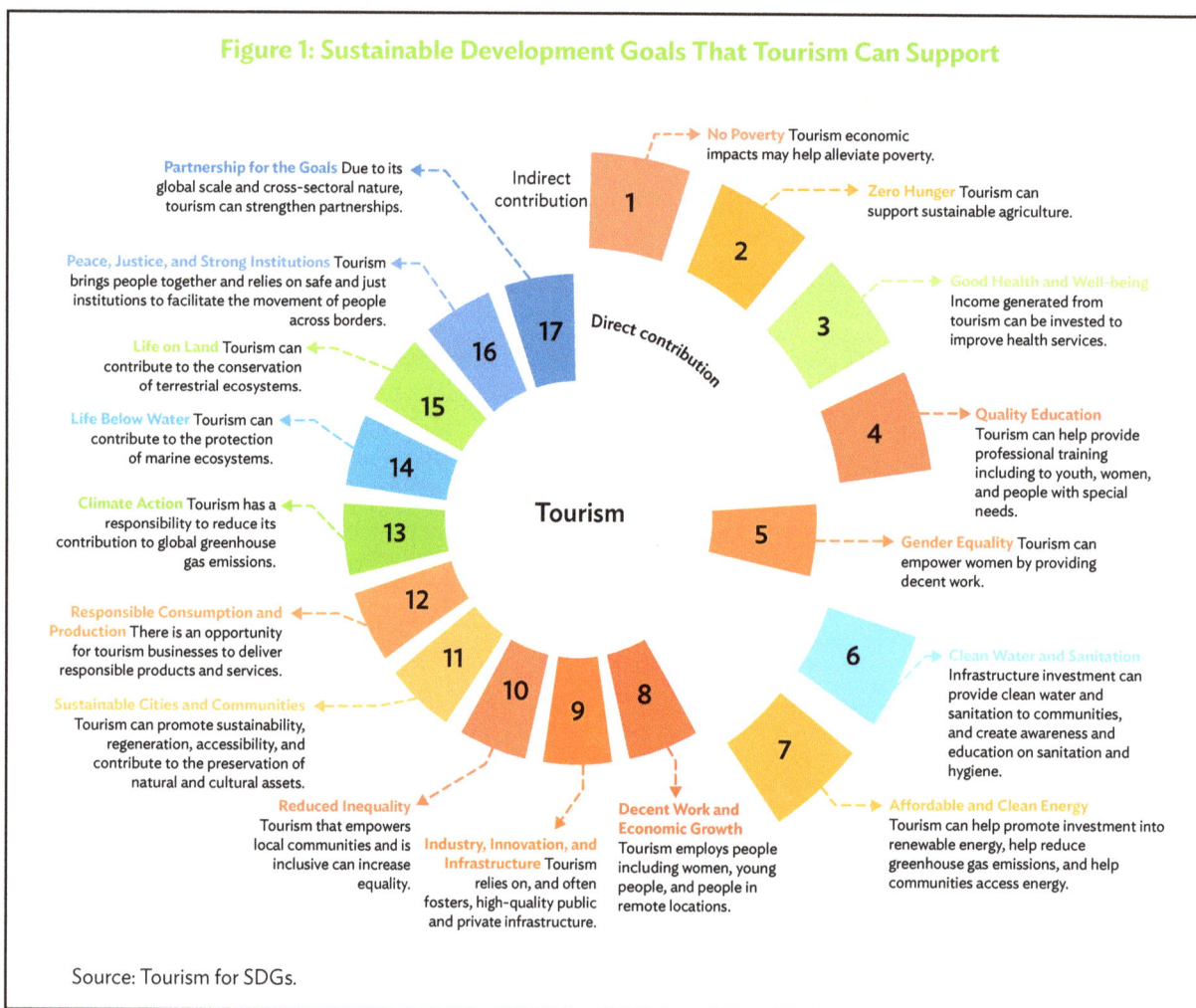

Figure 1: Sustainable Development Goals That Tourism Can Support

Partnership for the Goals Due to its global scale and cross-sectoral nature, tourism can strengthen partnerships.

Peace, Justice, and Strong Institutions Tourism brings people together and relies on safe and just institutions to facilitate the movement of people across borders.

Life on Land Tourism can contribute to the conservation of terrestrial ecosystems.

Life Below Water Tourism can contribute to the protection of marine ecosystems.

Climate Action Tourism has a responsibility to reduce its contribution to global greenhouse gas emissions.

Responsible Consumption and Production There is an opportunity for tourism businesses to deliver responsible products and services.

Sustainable Cities and Communities Tourism can promote sustainability, regeneration, accessibility, and contribute to the preservation of natural and cultural assets.

Reduced Inequality Tourism that empowers local communities and is inclusive can increase equality.

Industry, Innovation, and Infrastructure Tourism relies on, and often fosters, high-quality public and private infrastructure.

Decent Work and Economic Growth Tourism employs people including women, young people, and people in remote locations.

Affordable and Clean Energy Tourism can help promote investment into renewable energy, help reduce greenhouse gas emissions, and help communities access energy.

Clean Water and Sanitation Infrastructure investment can provide clean water and sanitation to communities, and create awareness and education on sanitation and hygiene.

Gender Equality Tourism can empower women by providing decent work.

Quality Education Tourism can help provide professional training including to youth, women, and people with special needs.

Good Health and Well-being Income generated from tourism can be invested to improve health services.

Zero Hunger Tourism can support sustainable agriculture.

No Poverty Tourism economic impacts may help alleviate poverty.

Indirect contribution

Direct contribution

Tourism

Source: Tourism for SDGs.

To enable a systematic assessment of the impacts and opportunities associated with COVID-19, the report develops an analytical framework to capture key dimensions of tourism (Figure 2). The framework builds on models that look at tourism in the context of visitors, industry, community, and the environment (VICE) (Sleeman and Simmons 2004). The framework in this report adds to the VICE model by considering factors that can help achieve the SDGs and ensure tourism activities remain within global and local carrying capacities (Rockström et al. 2009).

Figure 2: Sustainable Tourism Framework to Assess Contributions to the Sustainable Development Goals

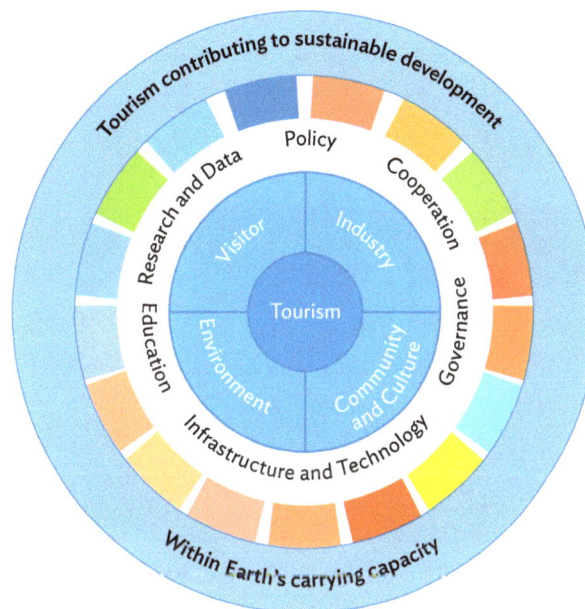

Source: Authors.

2 Pre-COVID-19: Tourism and Sustainable Development in Asia and the Pacific

This chapter describes growth in the tourism industry and how the sector contributed to achieving the SDGs before COVID-19. It examines different dimensions of the tourism industry through the VICE model, describing how the visitor, industry, community, and environmental dimensions of the tourism sector can be meaningfully integrated into development planning; and conversely, how development planning can support sector growth.

The Visitor Dimension

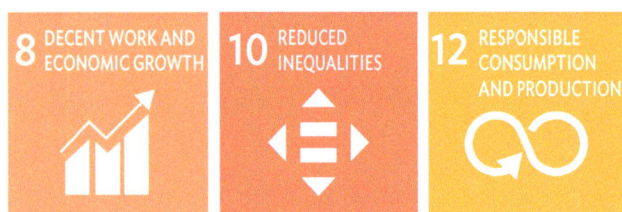

The "visitor" dimension of the VICE model considers who travels, where, and how they do so. This is most relevant to SDG 8 (decent work and economic growth), SDG 10 (reduced inequalities), and SDG 12 (responsible consumption and production). Visitors generate expenditures, jobs, and income, which support SDG 8, particularly in rural communities. The visitor dimension is also relevant to SDG 10, as increased visitor arrivals and the associated demand for transport services can improve access to mobility. The way visitors behave, and whether they consume responsibly, has impacts on communities and the environment, which relates to SDG 12 (Goodwin 2012). Key patterns and trends of visitors to consider include the following:

(i)   **International and domestic tourism.** Considerable growth in tourism over the 2010s increased economic opportunity but also increased reliance on international arrivals. Some countries are beginning to develop domestic markets in response.
(ii) **Market segments.** There is increasing recognition that different market segments bring different "value" to destinations. However, there are insufficient tools and strategies in place for targeting and attracting particular visitor groups effectively.
(iii) **Travelers and the environment.** Tourists are showing a growing interest in environmental sustainability, but there is limited information on how this translates into action.

Tourism Growth and Market Segments

In 2019, there were about 1.5 billion international tourists, and Asia and the Pacific was one of the fastest growing regions for tourist arrivals. From 2006 to 2019, international arrivals more than doubled to 364 million, and recent growth was particularly strong, with countries in Asia (including Maldives and Myanmar) recording double-digit growth from 2018 to 2019 (UNWTO 2021).

However, when considering the impacts of visitor arrivals on sustainable development (and SDG 8 in particular), it is important to consider several factors beyond international arrival statistics. For instance, the origin of travelers (whether they are domestic or international) and the tourism market segment (such as business or leisure) can impact their economic contributions and the resilience of a given market to local and external shocks.

Before COVID-19, many countries focused on promoting international tourism. This is evidenced by investments in international marketing and product development geared toward international visitors. International tourism results in foreign exchange earnings and input into the national economy, which makes it attractive to the public sector. However, domestic tourism volumes often outweigh international arrivals. Furthermore, arrival data highlights that shocks (such as extreme weather events) can create significant volatility, particularly for international arrivals. As such, a higher ratio of domestic against international travelers can increase the resilience of tourism industries to external shocks (Becken and Pant 2019). Despite the importance of domestic tourism to market growth and resilience, many countries know little about their existing or potential domestic markets. Further work also remains to increase visa equality and access to global mobility, in support of SDG 10 (Box 1).

Box 1: Visa Inequality

Visas are an important factor that affects where travelers hail from, and their access to mobility. Research indicates persistent issues of unequal access to visa privileges for citizens of different nations. Using information from Australia, New Zealand, the United Kingdom, the United States, and the Schengen Group, researchers have explored how passport holders from India, the People's Republic of China (PRC), Thailand, and Viet Nam, are affected. The study reveals that visa policies are primarily driven by economic (and subsequently), political, cultural, and even airport operational reasons. The analysis reveals that the PRC passport holders enjoy greater freedom to travel than, for example, travelers from India and Viet Nam. Disadvantages relate to visa costs, processes, and biometric requirements. Greater transparency is required to balance national interests with equal access to mobility for visitors, as indicated in the Sustainable Development Goals. The coronavirus disease (COVID-19) pandemic has the potential to exacerbate inequalities, especially if vaccine access remains imbalanced globally.

Sources: T. D. Pham et al. 2020. Visa Policies and Tourist Mobility of Asian Markets: Key Challenges and Determinants. Tourism Management Perspectives. Unpublished; and Authors.

Whether international or domestic, it is also important to note that there is no direct correlation between the number of visitor arrivals and economic growth. For instance, the People's Republic of China (PRC) recorded a 7% increase in international arrivals from 2018 to 2019, while expenditures decreased by 12% during the same period. Market segments can significantly affect the economic benefits of tourism in each country. For instance, business travelers generally spend more than tourists in other market segments, and as such, it may be useful for countries to identify the market segments of arrivals. Wellness tourism is another high-yield sector and has experienced considerable growth in recent years.

Box 2: Wellness Tourism

Wellness-related industries contribute 11% of economic output in Asia. Wellness tourism—which is a significant component of the wider industry—generated about $639 billion in 2017 globally, and $137 billion in Asia and the Pacific. The wellness tourism industry is growing twice as fast as other forms of tourism, and the yield of wellness visitors is considerably higher than that of other tourists. Several countries (including Bhutan, India, Malaysia, the People's Republic of China, the Philippines, and Sri Lanka) incentivize businesses setting up wellness programs. Sri Lanka and Thailand have wellness marketing strategies. Investments in the segment may prove beneficial following the pandemic when travelers are likely to be more health conscious. Wellness tourism diversifies visitor economies and spreads risks associated with concentrated market segments such as the vulnerability of beach tourism to climate change.

Sources: ADB. 2020. Asian Development Outlook 2020 Update: Theme Chapter: Wellness in Worrying Times. Manila; and Authors.

Countries may be even more interested in attracting high-spending visitors after the pandemic. However, there is a growing emphasis on the notion of "value." The consumer trend for organic products, health, and wellness provides a pertinent example of how a focus on quality helps achieve higher returns, as customers are willing to pay a premium. Some countries—such as Bhutan—have developed policies to manage growth and attract higher spending visitors. In Bhutan, visitors have to buy "minimum daily packages" ($250 per day) that cover local travel and a Bhutanese guide.

Visitor Behavior and Pledges

A growing number of tourists are demonstrating environmental awareness and interest in reducing the negative impacts of their travel (Higham et al. 2016). Accordingly, consumer pressure can improve the environmental sustainability of the tourism industry. However, it is still unclear as to what degree travelers are willing to change their behavior, pay higher prices for sustainable products, or support "better alternatives". The degree of environmental support travelers are willing to provide is also linked to how well the options are communicated to visitors (Warren et al. 2016).

One way to engage visitors is to provide a behavioral code or pledge. A visitor pledge is a form of communication that encourages the visitor to behave responsibly. The idea of visitor pledges builds on the United Nations World Tourism Organization (UNWTO) Global Code of Ethics for Tourism, which was adopted in 1999 as a comprehensive set of principles to guide tourism development. Several countries have developed codes that correspond to national and cultural values. Examples include the Palau Pledge and the Tiaki Promise in New Zealand.

In addition to codes or pledges, there are a growing number of options for tourists to offset their emissions with carbon credits. These are particularly useful in cases where emissions cannot be reduced directly. Several factors influence willingness to contribute to offset schemes, including awareness, knowledge, social norms, attitudes toward the environment, gender, and income (Choi and Ritchie 2014). Most carbon offset programs relevant to the tourism industry focus on aviation. The carriers in the region that offer carbon offsetting programs and disclose information on uptake include Air New Zealand, Cathay Pacific, Eva Air, Qantas, and Virgin Australia (Becken and Pant 2019). Some providers share information on the carbon footprint of a given journey (such as Skyscanner and Bookdifferent) and some include offset options in booking packages (Skift 2020). Despite some adoption, however, overall uptake is low.

Box 3: Aviation and Emission Reduction Frameworks

The Carbon Offset and Reduction Scheme for International Aviation (CORSIA) is the central framework for aviation sector emission reductions. CORSIA is under the leadership of the International Civil Aviation Authority and relies on carbon offsets to achieve carbon neutral growth.

Despite some progress on adoption, CORSIA has been criticized because it allows for the use of carbon credits issued in non-aviation sectors. While credits can offset emissions, they do not equate to physical emission reductions in the industry, leaving aviation as one of the largest sources of physical emissions.[a] The "zero sum effect" of compensating for emissions is often criticized because it does not achieve absolute reductions of atmospheric carbon concentrations.[b]

[a] J. Faber et al. 2020. International Aviation and Shipping. *Emissions Gap Report 2020*. Nairobi: United Nations Environment Programme.
[b] S. Becken and B. Mackey. 2017. What Role for Offsetting Aviation Greenhouse Gas Emissions in a Deep-Cut Carbon World? *Journal of Air Transport Management*. 63. pp. 71–83.
Sources: Authors' compilation.

The Industry Dimension

The "industry" dimension of the VICE model considers all business aspects of tourism. This is most relevant to achieving SDG 1 (no poverty); SDG 5 (gender equality); SDG 8 (decent work and economic growth); SDG 9 (industry, innovation, and infrastructure); and SDG 12 (responsible consumption and production). Tourism can help alleviate poverty and contribute to economic growth, leading to a redistribution of wealth and investment in less developed economies. However, several core remaining questions need to be addressed by the broader industry, such as who reaps the benefits, and how business activity in tourism affects sustainability. Key themes include the following:

(i)   The economic benefits of tourism are not often distributed evenly across businesses of different sizes, communities, and other stakeholders.

(ii)   The tourism sector offers a wide range of jobs and skill development opportunities, but there are persistent skills shortages, issues related to labor rights for migrant workers, and inequality.

(iii) Gender inequality remains a challenge for tourism labor markets, with women more often participating in the informal economy than men and experiencing disproportionate impacts from crises.

(iv)   There are emerging opportunities for tourism businesses to engage in environmental protection, such as by entering certification schemes and managing energy and water resources more efficiently.

Several programs help businesses become more efficient, but overall—and due to growth—the footprint of the tourism industry is growing.

Economic Contributions

Most tourism businesses, by volume, are micro, small, and medium-sized enterprises (MSMEs). However, their overall capital outlay contributes less than larger businesses (APEC 2019). This often means that industry-wide decisions are made by relatively few large players and that MSMEs must work within the context of these decisions. The tourism industry consists of many subsectors, including transport, accommodation, tour operators, food and beverage, and attractions. It also relies on support services, infrastructure, and a range of organizations (Chapter 2.5) Achieving sustainability across the broader industry requires adjustments across the full value chain.

Tourism sectors in Asia and the Pacific have seen sustained expansion over the past 30 years, and as a result, many stakeholders have come to take growth as a given. Governments have generally taken a laissez-faire approach—imposing limited restrictions on growth and sector development—and at the same time, many businesses have become inert to innovation. This growth model required little sophistication at the government level and limited business innovation to attract guests, as the throughput of visitors was certain. In the wake of COVID-19, however, businesses will increasingly find the need to innovate to compete for a smaller pool of visitors. Governments will need to formulate policies that encourage growth while managing development to be economically and environmentally sustainable.

While policymakers in developing economies often place poverty alleviation as a core objective of their tourism industries, it is difficult to measure the primary and secondary economic contributions. The Tourism Satellite Account (TSA) is a tool used to measure the economic contribution of the tourism industry and its subsectors. However, the specific subsectors included in this measure vary considerably. India, for example, includes leather footwear, gems, and jewelry in its TSA, since tourists often purchase these products (UNESCAP 2019). Within the TSA framework, the gross domestic product (GDP) of the tourism sector is the most appropriate measure to reflect its contribution to a domestic or regional economy. This measure provides the amount of domestically produced output that visitors consume. High contributions to GDP indicate high tourism dependence (UNWTO 2020). For example, tourism contributes 48% to GDP in Macau, China; 38% in Maldives; 26.3% in Georgia; 13% in Fiji; and 9% in the Philippines. The gross value added per tourism employee (a measure of labor productivity) is also used to assess the economic impact of tourism (Pham 2019).

Box 4: Who Benefits from Tourist Expenditures

Most countries measure tourism expenditures (money spent by visitors) to assess the economic impact of tourism. This can be used to understand the multiplier of each dollar spent in a region, or how much each dollar circulates through the economy. Higher multipliers indicate better connected local supply chains. This, in turn, means that expenditure made by a tourist "at place" is likely to generate greater benefit for local people. In many destinations, a considerable share of tourism products (such as specialized food or drinks) is imported to satisfy visitor expectations. Such leakage is particularly evident in island economies and developing countries. A value chain analysis in Botswana, for example, shows that only 37% of visitor expenditures remain in the local community.

Even if leakage is low, it is not always clear who benefits from tourism within a community. There is a risk that those who already have access to power or capital receive disproportional benefits from tourism. There is space to explore additional measures to capture the genuine benefits of tourism on communities. For example, measuring the distribution of tourism revenue or the number of entrepreneurs in a community may be useful measures of the contribution of tourism to the Sustainable Development Goals.

Source: A. Rylance and A. Spenceley. 2017. Reducing Economic Leakages from Tourism: A Value Chain Assessment of the Tourism Industry in Kasane, Botswana. *Development Southern Africa*. 34(3). pp. 295–313.

Tourism Jobs

Before the pandemic, tourism—directly and indirectly—supported 150 million jobs (or 10% of total employment) in the Asia-Pacific Economic Cooperation region (APEC 2019). The share of tourism employment varies by economy, with tourism in some locations showing higher contributions to exports per employee, indicating higher labor productivity (Figure 3).

About 80% of tourism jobs are in MSMEs globally, and about half of these are in hotels and restaurants with fewer than 10 employees (APEC 2017). A study in Sri Lanka reported that tourism-related MSMEs performed better than nontourism-related MSMEs. The study revealed that the profit of tourism MSMEs was substantially higher, but the level of education of tourism MSME owners was slightly lower than that of nontourism ones (Deyshappirya and Nawarathna 2020). Furthermore, a substantial number of tourism jobs are part of the informal economy. In many countries in Asia and the Pacific, this can be as high as 75% of workers in the sector (ILO 2020).[1] Typically, these are not protected by labor laws, and—in times of crisis—they are likely to be the most vulnerable ones.

---

[1]   Informal workers are often not registered or licensed and participate in the "sharing economy."

Figure 3: Share of Tourism Jobs and Export Earnings in Asia and the Pacific, 2019

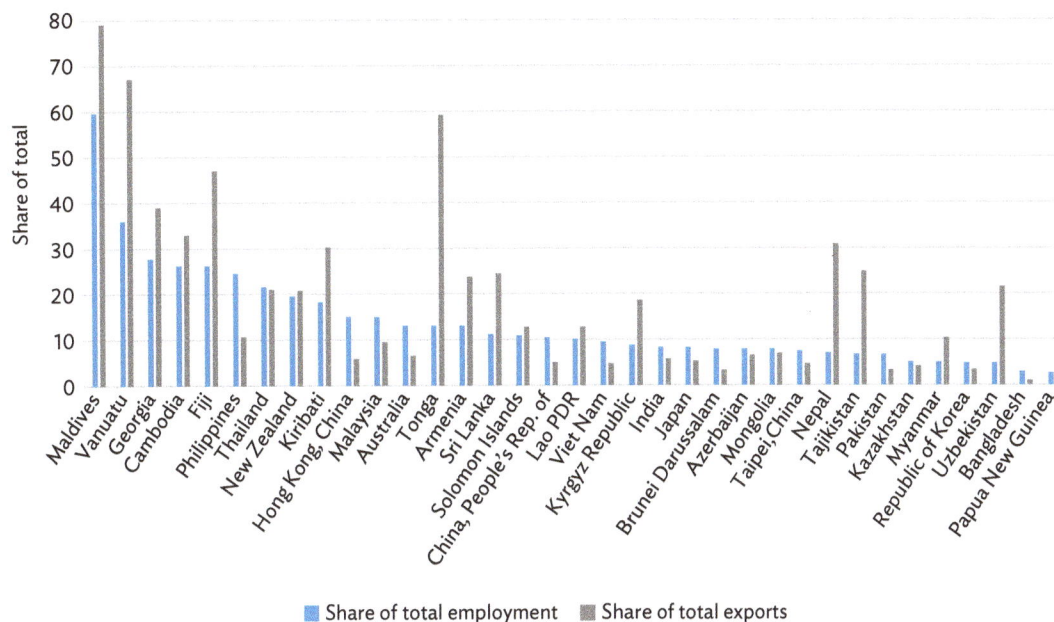

Lao PDR = Lao People's Democratic Republic.

Note: Figures do not differentiate migrant workers.

Source: World Travel and Tourism Council. 2020. *Economic Impact Reports.*

Many tourism jobs are paid poorly. For example, hospitality workers in Indonesia work 17% more hours than the national average and earn 17% less than the average wage (APEC 2017). Despite these challenges, tourism jobs can offer a range of new skills (Chapter 2.5). Understanding the range of skill training opportunities generated by tourism is important for advancing SDG 8 as it relates to decent work.

The tourism industry experiences a high degree of labor mobility in Asia as tourism workers in the region are driven by many factors, including economic conditions or lack of opportunity in their home country. Further, the hospitality sector in many countries relies on migrant workers, youth, and women, who accept low pay and low status work (Janta et al. 2011). The high share of migrants in the tourism workforce presents several challenges relating to workers' protection, visa arrangements, and the dependence of tourist destinations on external workforces; and the pandemic has significantly affected opportunities for migrant workers (Box 5). These factors are highly relevant for assessing whether tourism provides "decent work" in line with SDG 8. On the other hand, remittance payments made by overseas tourism workers constitute significant—and often existential—income for families at home, as well as for associated national economies. Whether this dependence is sustainable in the long term is not clear.

Gender Issues

Tourism has provided women access to economic and entrepreneurship opportunities that would not exist otherwise, and which can improve their lives and status through economic independence. SDG 5 emphasizes the access of women and girls to safety, education, employment, health care, and representation in leadership roles; while SDG 4, SDG 8, and SDG 16 also have significant gender dimensions.

Box 5: Critical Reflections on Human Rights and Tourism

There are several dimensions through which to consider human rights in the tourism industry. One includes sex tourism and its link to migration, human rights, sex trafficking, and the emotional dimensions of trauma. Tourism can only contribute to sustainable development if human rights become a category that is considered by all the stakeholders. To improve human rights in tourism, the International Tourism Partnership (ITP) has launched the first industry training to specifically focus on the risks of modern slavery in hotels. Hilton developed this training for their staff and made it available to other ITP members and the hotel industry more broadly.

Sources: A. Brooks and V. Heaslip. 2019. Sex Trafficking and Sex Tourism in a Globalised World. *Tourism Review*. 74 (5). pp. 1104–1115; and B. P. George and V. Varghese. 2007. Human Rights in Tourism: Conceptualization and Stakeholder Perspectives. *Electronic Journal of Business Ethics and Organization Studies*. 12(2). pp. 40–48.

However, progress on gender equity within the tourism industry has not reached its potential. Gender gaps persist as they relate to positions within a company, types of contracts, and pay. Women comprise 54% of the tourism workforce, but they are underrepresented in management roles and earn 14.7% less than men (UNWTO 2019). The pay gap is, in part, a result of lower positions; but may also reflect a broader gender bias. In addition, female staff and hospitality workers are at risk of gender-based violence and sexual harassment, which has been highlighted by the #MeToo movement (Ram 2018).

The share of female employment varies across countries and cultural contexts; with a portion of female workers being migrants, refugees, or international students. Women are overrepresented in part-time, casual, and seasonal jobs; and more likely to experience exploitation and poor conditions. Manual labor in hospitality is stereotyped as an extension of domestic care work, which women traditionally perform without pay. Front-facing service jobs rely on aesthetic, affective, and emotional labor, often provided by women (Coffey et al. 2018).

Although large tourism organizations have begun highlighting gendered employment issues and promoting equality as a corporate goal, there are persistent challenges concerning how gender gaps are measured, reported, and rectified.

There has been progress in female entrepreneurship in select subsectors—such as Airbnb accommodation—and there are opportunities to leverage this to catalyze further entrepreneurship and financial independence. There has also been progress with women in leadership roles—though gaps remain—and progress varies by organization and country. For example, in Papua New Guinea, most managerial roles in the tourism board are held by women. However, national systemic barriers to gender equality remain—such as maternity leave—which hampers broader female empowerment (UNWTO 2019).

Sustainability is typically associated with the environment and against this topic, gender equality receives relatively less attention. Similarly—and despite tourism being widely recognized as a vehicle for the empowerment of women—gender equality was not explicitly featured in the five key areas of the International Year of Sustainable Tourism for Development. More organizations are expressing commitment to SDG 5, but management practices remain patriarchal and continue to reproduce attitudes, traditions, and norms that privilege men. More needs to be done to achieve inclusive and equitable workplaces. Further, the narrative of gender issues has focused on economic empowerment. There is a need for more discussion on political empowerment and broader questions on structural inequalities.

Business Environmental Practices

Many tourism businesses are investing in environmental initiatives.[2] To avoid accusations of greenwashing, and to increase transparency and credibility, some businesses opt for sustainability certification. Certification programs include national voluntary schemes (such as Ecotourism Australia); mandatory national programs linked to the business licenses (such as Tourism Accreditation Vanuatu); regional or global programs (such as European Ecolabel for Tourist Accommodations, EarthCheck, and Green Key International); subsector certification programs (such as Biohotels or Ecocamping); and programs that focus on a specific area of sustainability (such as Airport Carbon Accreditation program).

The Global Sustainable Tourism Council (GSTC) provides best practice criteria for tourism businesses and destinations with affiliated certification schemes. GSTC covers areas such as (i) effective sustainable management, (ii) maximizing benefits and minimizing negative impacts on local communities, and (iii) preserving cultural heritage and the environment. GSTC provides certification and resources on conservation, reducing pollution, and conserving biodiversity, ecosystems, and landscapes (GSTC 2016). Certification programs are externally audited to ensure alignment with best practices and high quality standards.

Use of resources such as energy and water varies widely among tourism businesses (Warren and Becken 2016). For example, energy use in hotels in Taipei,China alone can range from 83 megajoules to 408 megajoules per guest night (Wang and Huang 2013). Many factors influence resource use, for example, occupancy, service levels, geography, and facility conditions and operational practices. Type of accommodation is a key factor because five-star hotels offer larger rooms and more facilities, many of which require more resources. Some hotels provide quality service while maintaining a small footprint.

Initiatives to reduce resource consumption do not have to involve expensive upgrades or retrofits (Warren and Becken 2016). Dusit Hotel in Bangkok, for example, saved an annual 5.4 million liters of water (about $2,900) by changing their laundry process (Griffith University 2014). Changing standard operating procedures, providing training, and creating awareness for all stakeholders (including guests) can achieve substantial savings (Warren et al. 2016). COVID-19 has triggered new interest in resource-saving programs as businesses look for opportunities to save on costs.

Community and Culture

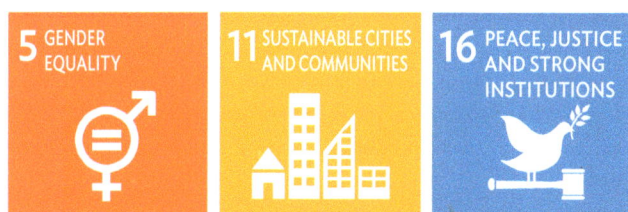

Tourism takes place in communities, whether they are urban or rural. The "Community and Culture" dimension of the VICE model considers all aspects of tourism that involve or affect local communities and their culture. This is most relevant to achieving SDG 5 (gender equality); SDG 11 (sustainable cities and communities); and SDG 16 (peace, justice, and strong institutions). Some of the central questions raised by Peter Keller in 1987 remain relevant today: "Development for whom? Development by whom? Development for what?" This

---

[2]   One example is the Hilton LightStay corporate responsibility management system.

chapter considers key patterns and trends in the tourism industry as they relate to communities and culture, such as the following:

(i)   Recent years have seen increasingly negative sentiment toward tourism, signaling a need for communities to have a greater say in its development.
(ii)   There is a growing focus on destination stewardship, encompassing all aspects of sustainable development, economic integration, and community well-being.
(iii)   Cultural assets are integral to tourist experiences, but tourism can erode tangible and intangible cultural heritage if not managed properly.

Community Perceptions of Tourism and Destination Management

"Overtourism" is when destinations suffer from visitor pressures to the detriment of locals or the environment. It often leads to negative public perceptions (Epler Wood et al. 2019). The key factors that shape public perceptions of tourism include (i) resident characteristics, like gender and education; (ii) intrinsic variables, such as the level of contact an individual has with tourists or their dependency on tourism; (iii) destination characteristics, like the type of tourism and how it is governed; and (iv) perceived impacts, such as infrastructure challenges and their impacts on quality of life. Managing perceptions and the impacts of tourism on communities requires good governance (Chapter 2.5).

Engaging with residents and community groups is essential to empowering local decision-makers in line with national or global interests. However, many local authorities have lost control of tourism development (Keller 1987). Also see Box 6 on community displacement. In recent years, tourism operators have begun to establish systems of co-management—for example with local or indigenous people—to govern natural resources and integrate tourism more comprehensively into local industries.

Box 6: Community Displacement and "Land Grab"

If not managed carefully, destination development and the influx of tourists can displace people and communities. A study on tourism in relation to land grabs notes that: "Tourism zoning, infrastructure development, and investor-friendly land legislation have paved the way for expansionist tourism development. Dispossession and displacement of local communities—often supported by the military or local security forces—are justified by invoking the 'public purpose' of tourism development for creating job opportunities, alleviating poverty, and protecting natural and cultural heritage sites."

While some land is taken without agreement by the local people—for instance, after natural disasters or conflicts—in some cases it is taken through tourism developments involving settlements. These are agreed on by local communities but are not always favorable to community development and future opportunities. One subtle form of displacement is residential tourism, where wealthy elites buy coastal properties for second home development. Impacts are often economic, but also affect livelihoods and well-being in the wider sense, especially when access to natural—and potentially spiritually important—resources is denied.

Sources: Authors; and A. Neef. 2019. *Tourism, Land Grabs and Displacement: A Study with Particular Focus on the Global South.* Auckland: Auckland University.

Community-based tourism is one way to diversify livelihoods in rural areas. A case study in the Lao People's Democratic Republic (Lao PDR) highlights the potential that tourism offers to some communities, but it also identifies challenges and potential unintended consequences that can undermine some of the SDGs (Pasanchay and Schott 2021). In particular, negative impacts on both the social and natural capital of a community run the risk of nullifying progress seen elsewhere. The study emphasizes the need for community-based tourism to take a whole-of-economy approach to avoid these risks. There are also sustainability certification programs (Green Destinations and EarthCheck Sustainable Destinations), and GSTC provides best practices that several certification schemes are aligned with (GSTC 2016).

Culture

Tourism builds on interactions between people and provides a vehicle for promoting intercultural dialogue and understanding among people from different cultures. Tourism can be a catalyst to revive cultures, including languages, customs, and traditions. At the same time, culture is an important attraction that drives tourism, evidenced by the large number of cultural sites visited by tourists. Pivotally, cultural and traditional practices can influence the sustainable management of resources, through tourism governance and decision-making (Box 7).

Box 7: Protecting Intangible Cultural Heritage

Intangible cultural heritage—like festivals and events—can support inclusive development. Diverse cultural traditions attract tourists, which can create employment and build a sense of place. However, to avoid potential negative impacts, tourism activities need to be ethical and responsible. This involves showing respect and safeguarding the intangible cultural heritage of local populations. To achieve this, locals should be the main beneficiaries of cultural tourism activities and should play a role in managing them. Behavioral guidelines can help avoid the commodification of cultural aspects.

The World Indigenous Tourism Alliance was founded in 2012 to empower indigenous communities involved in tourism. It provides a forum for indigenous people to share their traditional experiences and values. Tourism presents an opportunity to rebalance the harmony between different peoples, and between people and the environment.

Source: Authors.

There are 259 UNESCO World Heritage sites in Asia and the Pacific, of which 182 are cultural sites. Six sites are classified as "in danger" due to climate change, conflict, mismanagement, or overdevelopment (UNESCO 2018). Destinations profit from being recognized as UNESCO World Heritage sites. However, increased tourism can lead to consequences like overuse and unsuitable infrastructure developments.

Tourism growth also influences traditions and ways of life, potentially changing the local culture. Tourism development can lead to the abandonment of traditional practices, lower diversity, and increased reliance on tourism as a livelihood activity (Movono et al. 2018). For example, a study of Komodo Village on Komodo Island, Indonesia, revealed that the increased tourism resulted in the local community giving up fishing to focus on selling souvenirs. While this might deliver short-term gains, the dependence on this new livelihood brings considerable risks given that the market is limited, competitive, and seasonal (Lasso and Dahles 2018). In some countries, tourism can cause shifts from subsistence to cash economies, and consequently, reliance on cash earnings and disconnection from the land.

The Environmental Dimension

The environmental dimension of the VICE model considers how tourism interacts with ecosystems, climate change, and the built environment. This is most relevant to achieving SDG 13 (climate action), SDG 14 (life below water), SDG 6 (clean water and sanitation), and SDG 7 (affordable clean energy). This chapter examines the following key themes:

(i)   Tourism is at risk from climate change, especially when it takes place in high-risk or vulnerable areas, such as coastal regions.
(ii)   The carbon footprint of tourism is large and growing, but not easy to measure.
(iii)   Tourism generates waste and requires major changes to reduce the use of plastic. In many destinations, the water footprint of tourism is higher than the local communities.
(iv)   Tourism can protect or harm biodiversity protection, depending on how it is managed.

Climate Change

Climate impacts on tourism. Tourism often occurs in locations that are exposed to the impacts of climate change. The vulnerability of the tourism sector to climate change is mixed across Asia, with some countries—including Bangladesh, India, Myanmar, Pakistan, and Papua New Guinea—facing disproportionately high climate risk (Scott et al. 2019). It is critical to assess national risks and to build resilience accordingly.

The tourism sector in Thailand oversaw a detailed analysis of its climate risks, which assessed exposure and vulnerability against core hazards, including heat waves, floods, and sea level rise. The study found that ongoing investment in coastal areas increases the sector exposure to climate risk, while solving issues of seasonality and increasing domestic travel may reduce risks. Investing in knowledge, training, and climate policies for tourism development are other measures that can support resilience across the industry (Becken and Pant 2019).

Overall, climate change requires a multi-stakeholder governance structure that brings together the public and private sectors with communities to improve resilience (Government of Australia 2018). However, integrating climate policy into tourism development can be challenging due to conflicting goals (Chapter 2.5). For example, allowing further expansion of coastal resorts might provide short-term tourism revenue, but poses a long-term risk when sea levels rise, and extreme weather events threaten tourism assets and neighboring communities.

Impacts of tourism on climate change. Measuring climate impact on tourism needs to be a priority for governments and businesses alike. Governments need to track climate data in line with climate commitments, while businesses need to be aware of increasing carbon and climate risks, as well as voluntary environmental commitments. At an entry level, tourism firms and destinations should collect data on energy consumption and other sources of emissions. In 2008, UNWTO provided the first estimate of global emissions from the tourism sector, which found that tourism contributes about 5% of global fossil fuel-based emissions, with transport accounting for the largest share (Scott et al. 2008). A more recent study in 2018 used a different calculation method and found that the tourism sector contributes as much as 8% of man-made greenhouse gas (GHG) emissions, with transport, shopping, and food as the main contributors (Lenzen et al. 2018). Air travel is one of the largest contributors to global emissions, with associated GHG outputs steadily rising (Figure 4). At the same time, the centrality of air travel to the tourism industry (as well as to shipping and freight services) makes it difficult to redress core policy issues (Lee et al. 2020 and Faber et al. 2020).

Waste and Water

Unplanned urban development in coastal areas of Asia and the Pacific has contributed to inadequate management of solid waste and sewage, leading to extreme water contamination. Approximately 88% to 95% of total ocean plastic waste is attributed to 10 rivers in the region (The Mainichi 2018).

Figure 4: Carbon Dioxide Equivalent Emissions for Passenger Air Travel in 2015 and 2019

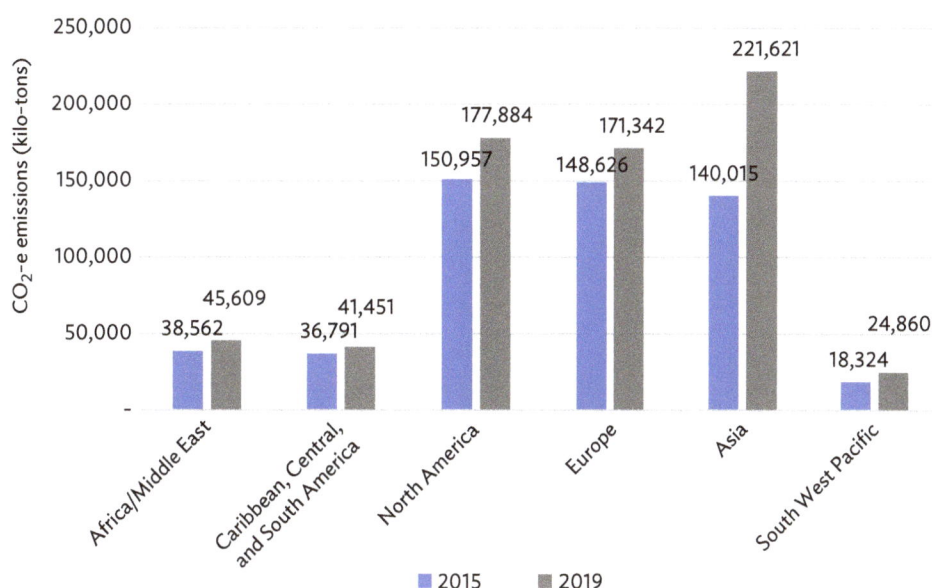

CO₂-e = carbon dioxide equivalent.
Source: Based on data provided by Amadeus IT and published in Becken and Shuker (2018).

The One Planet program of the United Nations Environment Programme recognizes tourism as a large contributor to plastic pollution and started the Global Tourism Plastics Initiative to rectify this challenge. While the exact share from tourism is unknown, evidence suggests that tourists contribute disproportionally. A study from the Langkawi Islands in Malaysia estimates that tourists generate almost twice the amount of solid waste per capita compared with locals (Shamshiry et al. 2011). Focusing on the Mediterranean, a World Wide Fund for Nature (WWF) study in 2018 found that tourists are responsible for a 40% increase in marine litter entering the Mediterranean Sea every summer, 95% of which is plastic.

Freshwater use by tourism is problematic in countries where water is scarce, and lack of access to freshwater often disproportionally affects women. The Aqueduct Water Risk Atlas by the World Resources Institute in 2019 provides an interactive tool for assessing different dimensions of water risk. The data highlight that large parts of Asia and Australia are exposed to extremely high overall water risk. This raises questions around supply, but also equity and fairness. Analysis of municipal water use and water use of tourists in Figure 5 shows that the estimated water use per person per day for tourists often exceeds that of residents (Becken 2014). For instance, in Bali, Indonesia, tourism consumes 65% of local water resources (Cole 2012).

Biodiversity

Uncertainty remains whether tourism has a net positive or negative impact on biodiversity. Tourism provides an impetus for countries to protect natural resources, ecosystems, and species. However, the impacts of travel can negatively affect habitats. Studies have demonstrated that the economic value of a species or habitat from tourism is greater than extractive alternatives.

Figure 5: Municipal Water Use, Minus Tourism-Related Consumption, and Estimated Water of Tourists

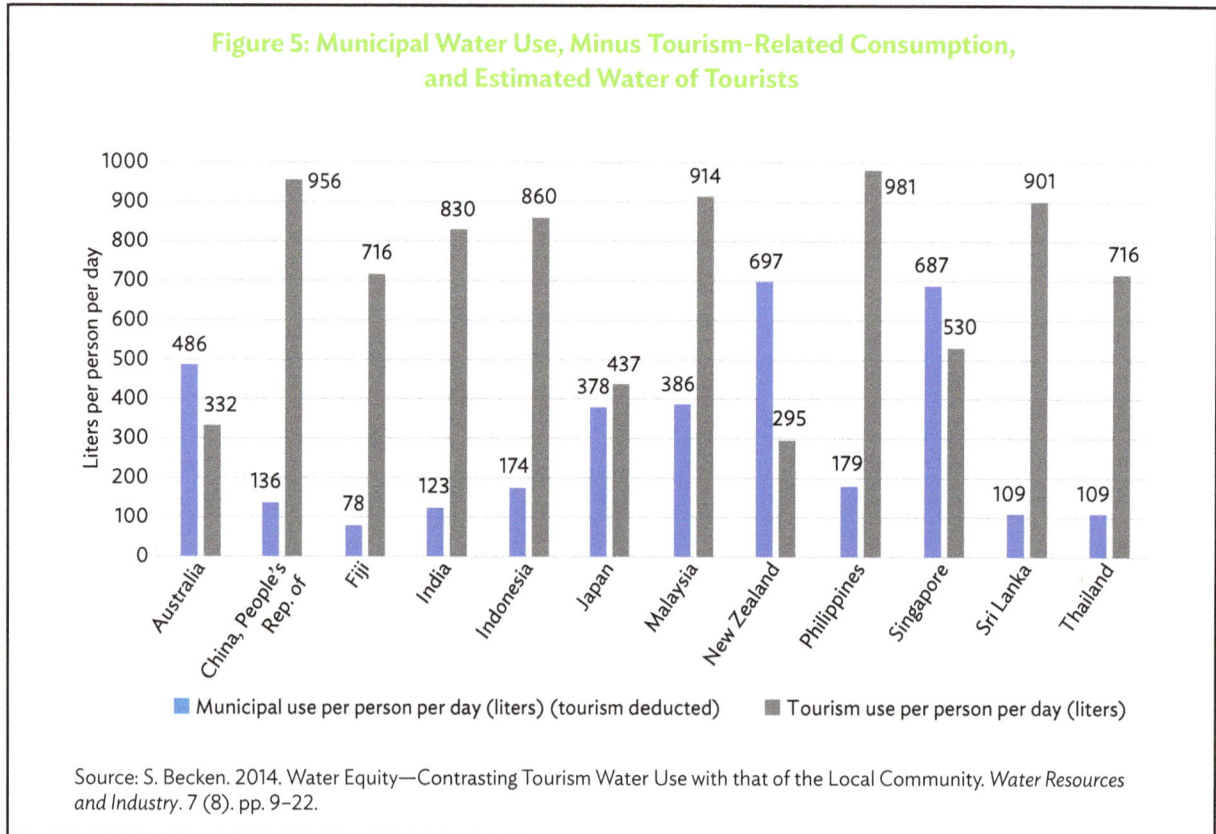

Municipal use per person per day (liters) (tourism deducted) ■   Tourism use per person per day (liters) ■

Source: S. Becken. 2014. Water Equity—Contrasting Tourism Water Use with that of the Local Community. *Water Resources and Industry*. 7 (8). pp. 9–22.

Box 8: Links between Biodiversity, Habitat Loss, and Pandemics

Scientists argue that the increasing loss of ecosystems and species increases the likelihood of pandemics. The World Wildlife Fund (WWF) compiled the following messages in response to the COVID-19 crisis:

(i)   Viruses, bacteria, and other microorganisms have played a vital role in life on Earth for 3.8 billion years. Many are essential for ecosystems and human health.

(ii)   A few microorganisms—such as pathogenic bacteria and viruses or parasitic protozoa—can have significant negative effects on human health. Pathogens can transform quickly, which allows them to pass from wild animals to humans.

(iii)   The chances of viruses passing from wild and domestic animals to humans may be increased by the destruction and modification of natural ecosystems, or the illegal or uncontrolled trade of wild species.

(iv)   Human behavior significantly increases these risks, and the speed with which humans travel between continents can cause the runaway spread of pandemics.

(v)   Conserving and maintaining nature and the benefits it provides are essential for preserving human health and well-being.

Source: World Wildlife Fund. 2020. *The Loss of Nature and the Rise of Pandemics: Protecting Human and Planetary Health*.

A recent example is the Mapping Ocean Wealth project by Nature Conservancy that highlights the importance of tourism to coral reef preservation (World Economic Forum 2017). In contrast, however, the Great Barrier Reef highlights a precarious link with tourism, in that carbon-intensive travel to visit the reef eventually contributes to its decline.

Enabling Factors

The success of tourism in contributing to sustainable development depends on a range of enablers. Opportunities exist to better integrate tourism with other policy domains (such as transport and the environment) and industries. Integration also needs to occur vertically across government levels, such as for infrastructure decisions and funding. Education, training, research, and investment in monitoring are other important enablers.

Governance and Cooperation

Governance structures comprise knowledge sharing and the application of power, resources, and rules to a given industry. They also include cooperation and coordination among stakeholders in both the public and private sectors. The distribution of power at multiple levels is at the heart of governance (Hall 2007). Cooperation and delegation of roles within countries and across regions are essential to effectively govern the tourism industry. A key challenge for tourism governance is that the industry is often not a priority for top decision-makers. As a result, there is little dialogue on tourism at the highest levels of government, though this may change due to COVID-19. With limited government intervention, tourism has historically been self-regulated by industry stakeholders.

Introducing long-term planning and clear objectives to higher levels of government can support stronger governance across the industry, and in turn enable tourism stakeholders to collaborate toward achieving SDG impacts. Some of the following principles of good societal governance are relevant to the tourism sector and associated governance.

(i)   **Participation:** Everyone should have a voice in decision-making, either directly or through legitimate intermediate institutions that represent their interests.
(ii)   **Rule of law:** Legal frameworks should be fair and enforced impartially.
(iii) **Transparency:** Information should be freely available. Processes, institutions, and information should be directly accessible to those concerned with them.
(iv)   **Responsiveness:** Institutions and processes should seek to serve all stakeholders.
(v)   **Consensus orientation:** Good governance mediates potentially conflicting interests to reach a broad consensus on what is in the best interests of the group.
(vi)   **Equity:** Everyone should have opportunities to improve or maintain their well-being.
(vii) **Effectiveness and efficiency:** Processes and institutions should seek to produce results while making the best use of resources.
(viii) **Accountability:** Decision-makers should be accountable to the public, as well as to institutional stakeholders, internally and externally.

Some governments in Asia and the Pacific have stand-alone tourism ministries, while most combine tourism with ministries of culture or the economy. Given the crosscutting nature of tourism, some governments have established interministerial groups (Figure 6).

Figure 6: Tourism in Government Agencies

Foreign Affairs
Singapore, Turkmenistan, Uzbekistan

Transport/ Infrastructure
Bangladesh, Japan, Kiribati, Taipei,China

Economy and Trade
Armenia, Australia, Fiji, Georgia, Myanmar, New Zealand, Tuvalu

Culture
Azerbaijan, People's Republic of China, Kyrgyz Republic, Lao People's Democratic Republic, Malaysia, Nepal, Papua New Guinea, Republic of Korea, Solomon Islands, Timor-Leste, Viet Nam

Tourism
Bhutan, Cambodia, India, Maldives, Myanmar, Nauru, Pakistan, Philippines, Samoa, Tajikistan, Tonga, Vanuatu

Sport
Kazakhstan, Thailand

Environment or Primary Resources
Brunei Darussalam, Mongolia, Palau, Sri Lanka

Tourism Boards
Australia; Hong Kong, China; New Zealand; Palau; Samoa; Singapore; Thailand

Source: Authors.

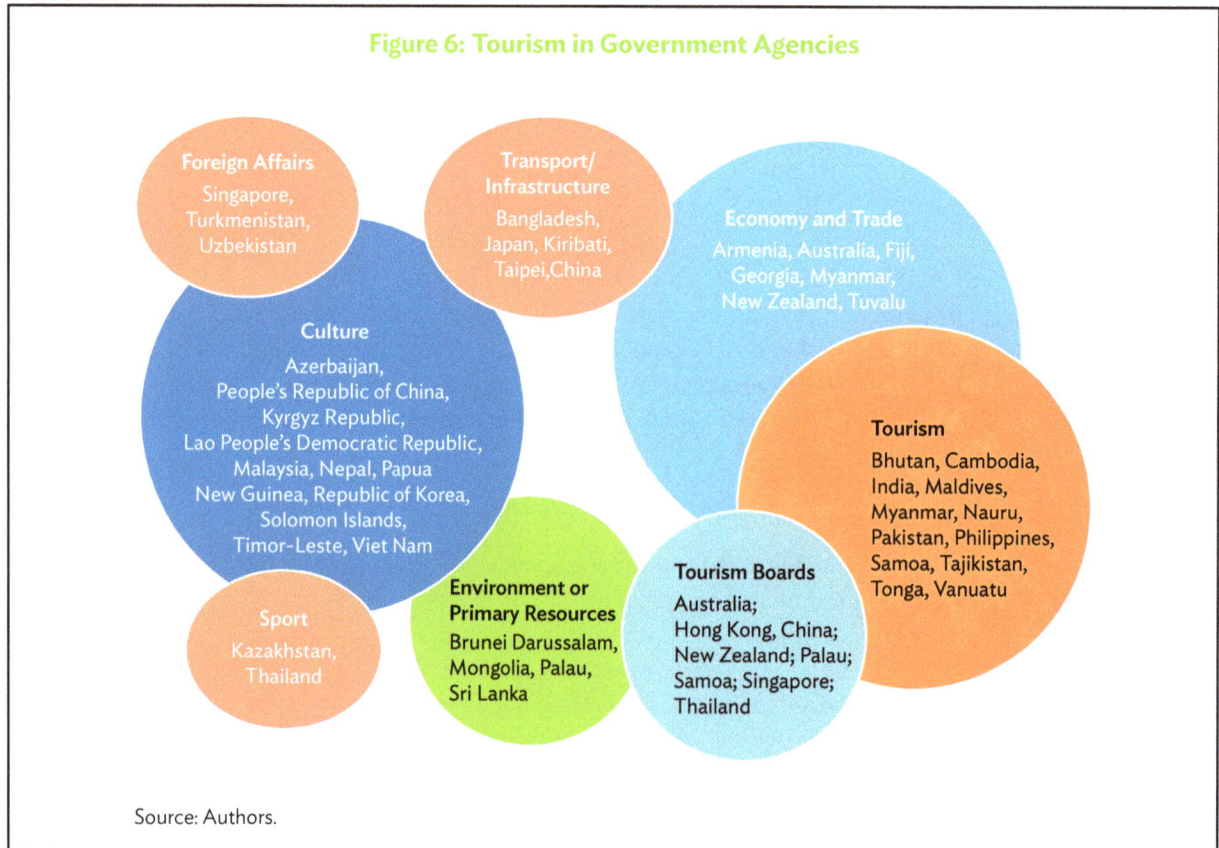

There are multiple layers of public sector involvement in the governance of tourism. Regional and local governments play a key role in planning, delivering, managing, and promoting tourism. Often, destination marketing organizations promote their region and—to a lesser extent—develop strategic plans for destination management. Destination marketing organizations are increasingly responsible for managing tourism impacts rather than just "selling a place". However, they often lack resources as tourism revenue is largely directed to central government agencies.

Government actors often work with nongovernment bodies—including industry associations, nongovernment organizations, community groups, and citizens—through public–private partnerships. Public–private partnerships bring together resources (including land, capital, knowledge, and skills) to effectively deliver sustainable tourism (UNWTO 2015). Cooperative efforts often focus on economic dimensions, which can be extended to cover environmental and social aspects. COVID-19 can either catalyze or disrupt such cooperation (Chapter 5: Future Pathways and Opportunities).

There is a difference between tourism finance and funding (Banhalmi-Zakar et al. 2016). Funding refers to money available for spending, which may or may not be subject to an agreement. For local governments, funding covers taxation, user charges, and grants. Typically, funding comes from government or development partners and does not always require repayment. Conversely, financing is typically provided by intermediaries, with the expectation of repayments and interest. Funding sources are often a prerequisite to demonstrate the viability of infrastructure projects to receive financing. Green finance—such as green bonds—is becoming more prevalent, though few examples exist in the tourism sector.[3]

---

[3]   Some examples include Etihad and JetBlue airlines, and Langham Hotel in Hong Kong, China.

Some types of cooperation see better results in regional groups. The Central Asia Regional Economic Cooperation (CAREC), for example, identifies tourism to foster economic activity and contribute to the SDGs (ADB and CAREC 2018). Similarly, the Greater Mekong Subregion (GMS) developed a joint GMS Tourism Sector Strategy (2016–2025).

Box 9: Good Governance—Carbon Reduction Success at Hong Kong International Airport

Good governance can be implemented by either the public or private sector, or a combination of the two. Deep decarbonization at the Hong Kong International Airport (HKIA) demonstrates the ability of a central authority to guide robust stakeholder collaboration to achieve shared sustainability goals.

The Airport Authority Hong Kong (AAHK) and its business partners pledged to make HKIA the greenest airport in the world. Before the pandemic, HKIA served 70.5 million passengers and handled 4.52 million tons of cargo annually. The airport has achieved measurable success in reducing carbon emissions. In 2016, the AAHK Board approved a second carbon pledge to further reduce the HKIA carbon intensity by 10% by 2020 relative to 2015. HKIA also operates a range of sustainability programs including staff awards, and partnerships with nongovernment organizations.

The AAHK approach is unique in that it focuses on collaborative airport-wide solutions to reduce its environmental footprint. Some 73,000 staff from a range of sectors working on the airport island are exposed to the sustainability initiatives of HKIA, providing a considerable multiplier effect.

Source: Authors.

ADB is one of the key organizations supporting cooperation in Asia and the Pacific. Although its sovereign lending does not have a stand-alone tourism project category, both ADB and the World Bank still invest in tourism. Table 1 maps tourism projects undertaken by ADB and the World Bank since 2010, including those classified as infrastructure, agriculture, finance, and water, highlighting the crosscutting nature of tourism. Designating

Table 1: ADB and World Bank Tourism Projects Since 2010

CRITERIA	ADB	WORLD BANK
Projects with the keyword "tourism"	125	187
Tourism-focused	24 (word "tourism" in both the title and the Design and Monitoring Framework)	42
Active tourism-related projects	33 (14 explicitly on tourism)	99 (40 explicitly on tourism)
Geographic coverage	Asia and the Pacific	Worldwide
Themes and/or enabling factors	Infrastructure; Research; Governance; Cooperation; Policy	Private Sector Development; Human Development and Gender; Environment and Natural Resource Management; Finance; Urban and Rural Development
Related sectors	Agriculture, natural resources, and rural development; Energy; Finance; Education; Public sector management; Health and social protection; Transport; Water and urban infrastructure and services	Industry, trade, and services; Social protection; Agriculture, fishing, and forestry; Finance; Water supply, sanitation and waste management, etc.

Sources: ADB. Projects and Tenders; World Bank. Projects (accessed 8 August 2020).

a dedicated tourism category in the future may lead to more effective investment in sustainable tourism. Development partners may consider other mechanisms to integrate tourism considerations into projects and to leverage shared resources across projects of different categories.

Box 10: The Almaty–Bishkek Economic Corridor

Considering the multicountry nature of tourism, regional approaches are effective for supporting sustainable development. The area between Almaty in Kazakhstan and Bishkek in the Kyrgyz Republic is characterized by rich cultural and natural heritage. There is considerable tourism potential, but development has been limited. The Almaty–Bishkek Economic Corridor (ABEC) Tourism Master Plan identifies opportunities for tourism attractions and prioritizes investments—such as ski resorts—along the mountain range between Almaty and Issyk-Kul, and links these winter sports facilities with summer tourism opportunities. It also proposes transport infrastructure improvements, including enhancing Almaty International Airport as the major gateway to the region. The ABEC plan highlights the importance of linking multiple enabling factors—in this case, tourism planning and infrastructure investment—through regional cooperation.

Source: ADB. 2019. *Improving Education, Skills, and Employment in Tourism–Almaty-Bishkek Economic Corridor.* Manila.

Policy

Much of the literature on tourism policy focuses on economic dimensions, like the benefits of deducting a goods and service tax for visitors in Singapore (Meng et al. 2013). However, there is limited research that focuses on sustainable tourism policy. Figure 7 illustrates five areas that governments can expand on to support sustainable tourism (Velasco 2016). The blue boxes show traditional areas, and the green ones show how they can be expanded to support the SDGs.

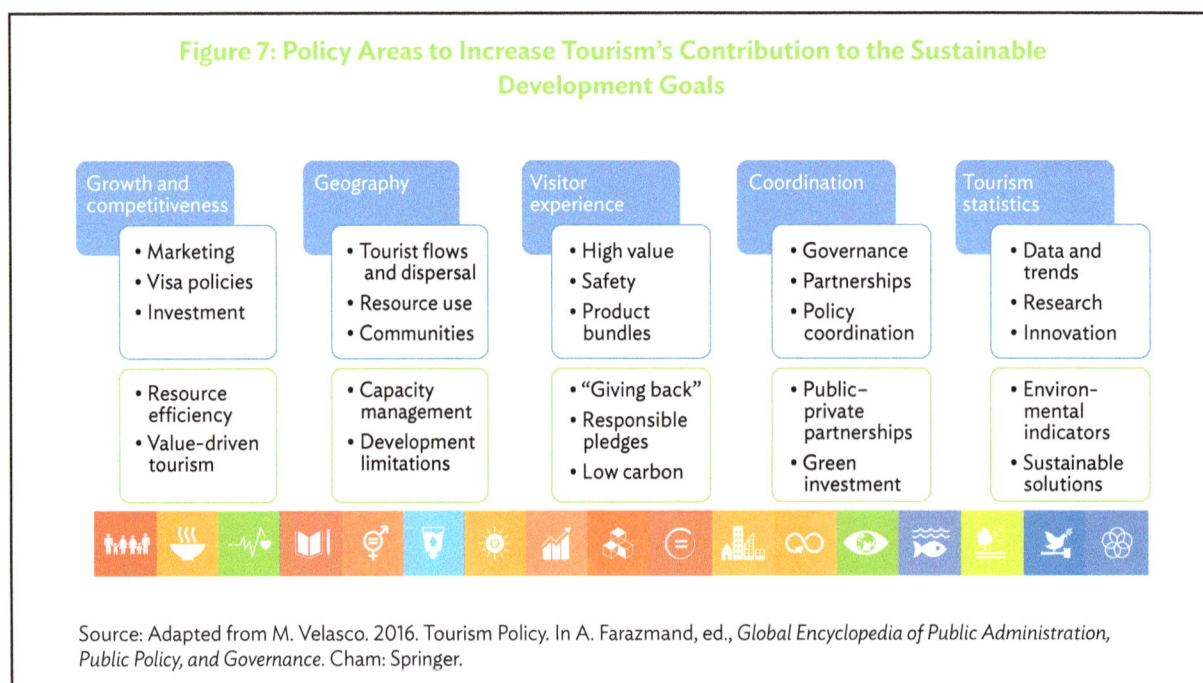

Figure 7: Policy Areas to Increase Tourism's Contribution to the Sustainable Development Goals

Growth and competitiveness	Geography	Visitor experience	Coordination	Tourism statistics
• Marketing • Visa policies • Investment	• Tourist flows and dispersal • Resource use • Communities	• High value • Safety • Product bundles	• Governance • Partnerships • Policy coordination	• Data and trends • Research • Innovation
• Resource efficiency • Value-driven tourism	• Capacity management • Development limitations	• "Giving back" • Responsible pledges • Low carbon	• Public–private partnerships • Green investment	• Environmental indicators • Sustainable solutions

Source: Adapted from M. Velasco. 2016. Tourism Policy. In A. Farazmand, ed., *Global Encyclopedia of Public Administration, Public Policy, and Governance.* Cham: Springer.

In 2005, the United Nations Environment Programme and UNWTO proposed five instruments to manage tourism impacts:

(i)   measurement instruments, including indicators and monitoring;
(ii)   command and control instruments, including legislation, regulation and licensing, land-use planning, and development control;
(iii)   economic instruments, including taxes, charges, and financial incentives;
(iv)   voluntary instruments, including guidelines and codes of conduct, reporting and auditing, and voluntary certification; and
(v)   support through capacity building, marketing, and information sharing to assist businesses and tourists in making activities more sustainable.

Master plans are an important instrument for tourism policy. Most ADB members—both from the Asia and the Pacific region and outside it—have developed tourism strategies. However, only 16% of ADB members mention the SDGs in their tourism strategy. The Sri Lanka Tourism Strategic Plan 2017–2020 has the most comprehensive references to the SDGs. Many of the plans that do not mention the SDGs were written before the SDGs but still mention sustainability. Overall, about 80% of national tourism plans include either a reference to the SDGs, sustainable development, or sustainability.

To address crosscutting issues such as climate change, health, and sustainable development, tourism policies need to be integrated across multiple portfolios. Effective representation of tourism in other portfolios is important for allocating funding and finance. Thailand, for example, allocates a budget specifically for policy integration and crosscutting issues, and its Ministry of Tourism and Sport has identified the opportunity to seek funding related to tourism and climate change.

In 2020, all but three of 68 ADB members submitted Voluntary National Reviews, and 45 mentioned tourism (UNWTO and UNEP 2017). The analysis highlights that most reports specifically link tourism to one or more SDG. Figure 8 shows the number of ADB members that identified how tourism contributes to achieving specific SDGs (for example SDGs 8, 12, and 15), but also how tourism poses a risk to SDGs if not managed (such as SDGs 12, 14, and 15). In addition, many reviews highlighted that tourism success is reliant on progress in many of the SDGs (such as SDGs 13, 14, and 15).

Climate change policies are also relevant to the tourism sector (Becken and Pant 2019). Under the Paris Agreement, countries are required to submit nationally determined contributions (NDCs) outlining their priorities for addressing climate change. Out of all ADB members, 66 submitted NDCs, but only 14 of them mention tourism.[4] In some cases, mentioning tourism might merely refer to its contribution to the economy, rather than meaningful climate action. Most countries that mention tourism in their NDCs are small island developing states, which often rely economically on tourism and are highly vulnerable to climate impacts. Including tourism in NDCs can assist in attracting finance for adaptation measures.

Infrastructure and Technology

Investing in either hard infrastructure (like roads and airports) or digital infrastructure is one of the major pathways for governments to intervene in tourism. The World Economic Forum (WEF) provided an analysis of tourism growth and quality of infrastructure, finding that many Southeast Asian countries have outgrown

---

[4]   The 14 countries are Armenia, the Cook Islands, Kiribati, Maldives, Nepal, Niue, Norway, Samoa, Solomon Islands, Sri Lanka, Thailand, Tonga, Vanuatu, and Viet Nam.

Figure 8: Reference to Tourism in Voluntary National Reviews

Number of ADB members

	0	5	10	15	20	25	30	35	40

1 No Poverty
2 Zero Hunger
3 Good Health and Well-being
4 Quality Education
5 Gender Equality
6 Clean Water and Sanitation
7 Affordable and Clean Energy
8 Decent Work and Economic Growth
9 Industry, Innovation, and Infrastructure
10 Reduced Inequality
11 Sustainable Cities and Communities
12 Responsible Consumption and Production
13 Climate Action
14 Life below Water
15 Life on Land
16 Peace, Justice, and Strong Institutions
17 Partnership for the Goals

■ Tourism contribution to SDGs   ■ Tourism negative effect on SDGs

ADB = Asian Development Bank, SDG = Sustainable Development Goal.
Source: United Nations. 2020. *Sustainable Development Knowledge Platform—Voluntary National Reviews Database.*

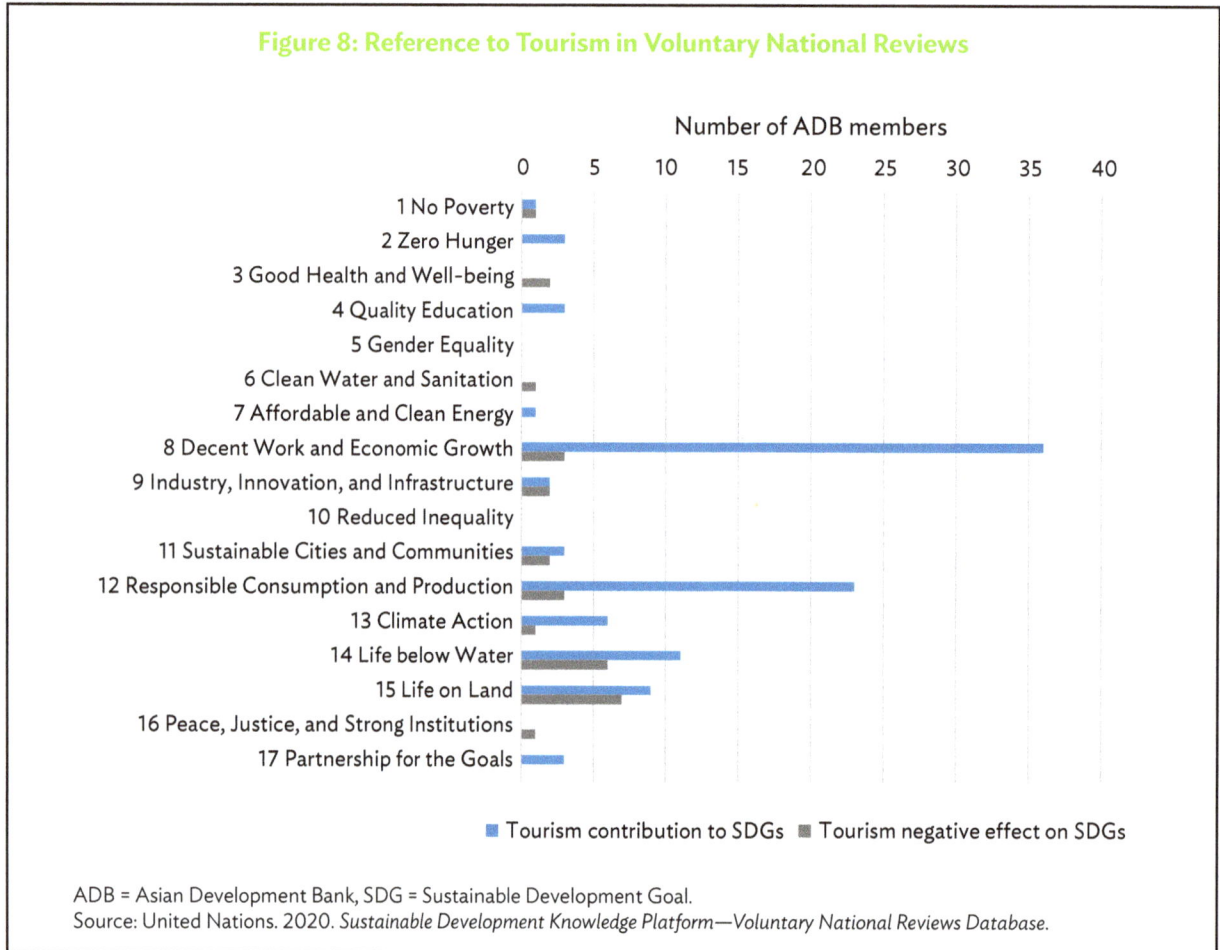

their infrastructure (Soshkin 2019). Airports are one example of hard infrastructure relevant to modern tourism. About half of international arrivals are now by air, and seven of the busiest 15 airports globally are now in Asia (UNWTO 2021 and Becken and Shuker 2018). Wastewater and solid waste management infrastructure are also highly relevant to sustainable tourism. In the absence of functioning treatment, it is difficult for individual companies to reduce their impact.

Digital infrastructure provides important support functions for the tourism industry, such as booking and communication systems. Tourists and suppliers may be disadvantaged if they lack sufficient digital infrastructure. WEF measured information and communication technologies (ICT) readiness as part of its travel and tourism competitiveness report (WEF 2019). In total, Asia and the Pacific scored 4.8 out of 7 points, with the top score of 6.6 received by Hong Kong, China. Countries with low ICT readiness scores include Pakistan (3), Bangladesh (3.3), and the Lao PDR (3.3). South Asia received a 3.5 average, which is well below the global average of 4.6.

Digital innovation in tourism has already changed many experiences, in particular augmented and virtual reality. Despite advances in digitalization, very little work has focused on improving sustainability through smart technologies to strengthen management practices, resource use, or influence guest behavior (Warren et al. 2018). An untapped opportunity exists to extend the application of smart technologies, for example by presenting smart meter data to guests, alongside information on how to reduce consumption.

Box 11: Biometrics and Using Digital Identities to Support Tourism

Biometrics and digital identities may provide more seamless and secure journeys. The concept involves capturing and uploading biometric and biographic data before their trip. Biometrics offer several benefits:

(i)   relieving pressure on airport and port infrastructure to reduce costs and enable travel growth;
(ii)   improving safety and security through improved authentication and reduction of fraud;
(iii)   enhancing customer satisfaction by eliminating bottlenecks across the journey; and
(iv)   integrating all touchpoints of the journey enabled by technologies.

While digital technology can provide substantial benefits—including for pandemic tracing—several barriers remain, including the need for global standards, consumer adoption, and data privacy.

Source: World Travel and Tourism Council. 2019. *Seamless Traveller Journey Emerging Models Overview and Findings Report.*

Research and Data

Tourism can benefit indirectly from advances in areas such as engineering or computer science, but connections need to be made through interdisciplinary approaches. Major questions remain on how much investment is going into tourism research, and the linkages between tourism research and sustainability (Epler Wood et al. 2019). This is the case for several reasons. First, tourism is not an identified discipline but instead falls under broader categories such as business, marketing, geography, or other areas. Second, although the region hosts some of the highest ranked universities in tourism and hospitality research, their research focuses on economic dimensions above sustainability.

Tourism research needs to be complemented by sound data programs and national tourism statistics. The Pacific Asia Travel Association provides a range of industry statistics and tools to inform decision-making in the region. UNWTO has catalyzed a global network of tourism observatories, as well as the Measuring Sustainable Tourism (MST) initiative. There are currently 11 MST pilot studies in Austria, Canada, Fiji, Germany, Italy, Mexico, the Netherlands, the Philippines, Saudi Arabia, Sweden, and Thailand. Samoa and Viet Nam have undertaken similar measurements aligned with the MST guidelines.

Communicating insights and data is critical. ADB's *Pacific Economic Monitor series* provides an excellent example of how high-level data on topical policy issues, such as climate change and COVID-19, can be made accessible in an engaging way (ADB 2020).

Box 12: The Ethics of Research on Digital Technology

Technology solutions have been developed rapidly to address some of the tourism-related challenges arising from the pandemic. At the same time, digital tourism researchers have raised alarms that the heavy use of digital technology might further exacerbate the digital divide, increase the vulnerability of people, breach privacy, and spread misinformation. While some tools support the ability to make mindful decisions, others have the potential to be manipulative or to undermine freedom and transparency. Thus, there is a crossroad in this research field to embrace or reject principles of historicity, reflexivity, transparency, equity, plurality, and creativity as digital technology advances.

Source: U. Gretzel et al. 2020. E-Tourism Beyond COVID-19: A Call for Transformative Research. *Information Technology and Tourism.* 22. pp. 187–203.

Education and Training

Strong growth in tourism in Asia and the Pacific brings with it demand for skilled workers. Attracting talented people and developing future leaders are critical for the industry. Although there are many tourism and hospitality degrees, apprenticeships, and vocational training and education programs, tourism businesses in the region continue to experience skill shortages. For example, the Almaty–Bishkek Economic Corridor region experiences a skills shortage of about 8,500 workers annually, covering both semi-skilled and higher qualified tourism workers (ADB 2019).

More broadly, shortages exist across all types of skill sets (Table 2). In developed economies, most respondents to an APEC survey perceived major and moderate shortages in hard skills (70%), and over 60% perceived a shortage of soft skills in graduates (APEC 2017). In developing economies, almost 80% of respondents perceived a major or moderate shortage in soft skills and about 75% in managerial skills. The gap in digital and ICT skills was smaller; maybe because recent graduates are better equipped with digital skills, or because some businesses perceive digital skills as less important.

Table 2: Different Types of Skills

Hard	Digital	Soft	Business	Analytical
Chef: Culinary technical skills	Accounts clerks: Accounting software	Language, literacy, and numeracy skills	Managerial skills	Researcher: Collecting and analyzing data
Sommelier: Wine skills	Airport staff: Airline software	Customer service skills	Problem solving and decision-making	Consultant: Analyzing context, communicating solutions
Airline Pilot: Aviation skills	IT administrator: System and software	Personal hygiene and presentation	Planning and organizing	
Beauty therapist: Different types of treatments	Marketing: Social media	Networking	Financial management Independent and teamwork	Planner: Spatial thinking

IT = information technology.
Source: Adapted from Asia-Pacific Economic Cooperation. *Developing the Tourism Workforce of the Future in the APEC Region.*

Soft skills are of particular concern to tourism businesses as they contribute to the quality service provided to guests (APEC 2017). These are also the skills that make tourism graduates valuable in other industries, especially service industries such as aged care. An underskilled workforce limits the competitiveness of the tourism sector, contributes to high staff turnover, and limits access to higher paid employment.

Often, MSMEs respond to skills shortage by investing in recruitment, rather than improving in-house training (APEC 2017). However, considering the cost of recruitment and onboarding, providing employees with development opportunities may not only be more cost-effective but also contribute to job satisfaction and retention. Sustainability should form part of tourism and hospitality training, providing the potential cobenefit of increased staff loyalty (Sourvinou and Filimonau 2018). Core issues impeding vocational training and education include low uptake of government training schemes (not because of lack of awareness), regulatory burdens associated with training programs, lack of funding or scholarships, and ties between industry and educators (APEC 2017).

3 COVID-19 Impacts and Responses in Asia and the Pacific

This chapter assesses the impacts of the pandemic on tourism. It draws on analyses by international organizations, consulting firms, and researchers, and includes expert insights from webinars and interviews. It is broadly structured around the four VICE components.

Decreased Travel Activity

In response to COVID-19, the UNWTO recorded the most significant decrease in international arrivals in the history of tourism, with 1 billion fewer international arrivals in 2020 than in the previous year, and an estimated loss of $1.3 trillion in export revenue (UNWTO 2021). In 2020, Asia and the Pacific experienced an 84% reduction in international arrivals (about 300 million), which is a higher loss than the global average of 74% (Figure 9).

Figure 9: Reduction in International Arrivals, 2020 (%)

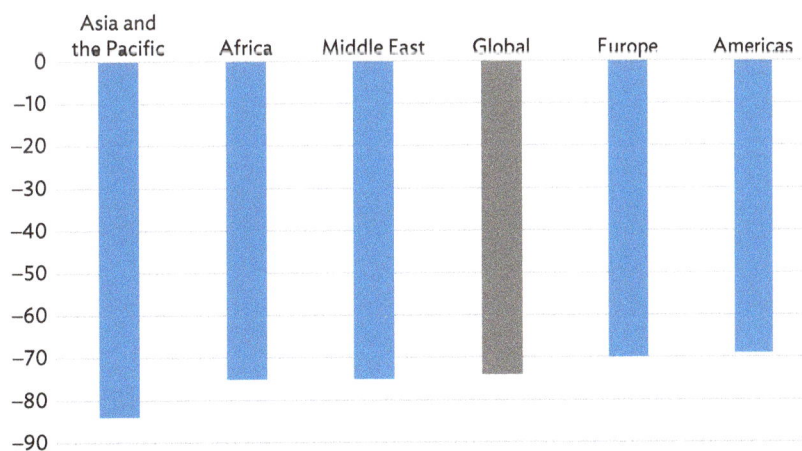

Source: United Nations World Tourism Organization. *2020: Worst Year in Tourism History with 1 Billion Fewer International Arrivals.*

Travel Restrictions and Airline Networks

Early in the crisis—at the end of April 2020—over 90% of the world was under full or partial travel restrictions. While some countries eased restrictions by the end of 2020, many remain in place as of September 2021. In December 2020, 27 destinations in Asia and the Pacific (59% of all destinations in the region) still had complete border closures in place, compared to 27% of countries worldwide (UNWTO 2020).

In December 2020, the International Air Transport Association reported that revenue passenger kilometers across all airlines decreased by 69.7% compared with December 2019 (International Air Transport Association 2020). When measured across the calendar year, 2020 traffic was down by 66% compared with the previous year. While there were some forward bookings, these declined again later in December 2020, because of increased travel restrictions in response to new waves of the pandemic, and more infectious mutations.

The occupancy rate of aircraft is an important performance indicator for the aviation industry. In 2020, the average passenger load factor across the industry was 17.8% lower than the 64.8% occupancy rate in 2019; and the average load factor for Asia and the Pacific dropped from 81.6% to 61.6% over the same period. This was despite dramatic reductions in available seat capacity. Most airlines retired a substantial part of their fleet (temporarily or permanently). This manifested in a 56.5% reduction of available seat kilometers from 2019 to 2020. Overall, the loss of 2,699 million passengers in 2020 equates to an economic loss of $371 billion in gross passenger operating revenues across airlines (ICAO 2021).

Signs of Recovery

Travel restrictions and limited air route networks affect all market segments, but some may rebound sooner than others. Recovery for destinations might rely on specific markets that are more likely to travel in the face of adversity, including the "visiting friends and relatives" segment, educational markets, and specialized workers. Leisure travel will follow, but business travel may be permanently reduced due to shifts in telecommunication (Becken and Hughey 2021). This has considerable repercussions for the whole industry, but particularly for convention centers, conference destinations, urban gateways, and full-cost airlines.

Economic Impacts

The widespread and long-lasting impacts of COVID-19 mean that tourism supply and demand will be affected in multiple ways and at compounding levels not experienced before.

Overview of Macro Indicators

Traditional econometric models that simulate changes in income and price sensitivity to derive demand are not suitable to capture complex COVID-19 effects such as consumer anxiety. Some sectors might be additionally affected by reputational repercussions, for example, the cruise ship industry.

Table 3 summarizes economic impacts, noting that impacts are not uniform. Regardless of how impacts are measured, the crisis will significantly reduce the ability of governments to invest in SDGs unless investments are made simultaneously through response and recovery packages. Unfortunately, only a small part (18%) of stimulus investment is classified as "green" (UNEP 2021). The numbers in Table 3 fail to convey the full extent of suffering in some destinations and by particularly vulnerable groups.

Table 3: Economic Impacts of COVID-19 to Date

Country	Impact	Description and Time of Publication
Samoa[a]	10.6% drop	Estimated loss to GDP from tourism receipts for FY2020 (April 2020)
Cook Islands, Niue, Samoa, Solomon Islands, Tonga, Vanuatu[b]	$2.3 billion	Estimated loss in tourism revenue for a 12-month period (May 2020)
Bangladesh[c]	$2.03 billion drop 420,000 impacted	Potential loss to GDP from travel and tourism earnings (June 2020) Estimated jobs at risk
Bhutan[c]	$2.2 million drop 50,000 (150,000) impacted	Loss in travel and tourism earnings (June 2020) Jobs at risk (with flow on impacts)
India[c]	$43.4 billion drop 9 million impacted 60% drop Complete shutdown	Potential loss to GDP from travel and tourism earnings (June 2020) Jobs at risk Closure of hotels MICE market
Maldives[c]	$700 million drop 35,000 impacted	Potential loss to GDP from travel and tourism earnings (June 2020) Jobs at risk
Nepal[c]	$460 million drop 230,000 impacted 20,000 impacted 2,600 impacted	Potential loss to GDP from travel and tourism earnings (June 2020) Jobs at risk Tour and trekking guides unemployed Trekking agencies closed
Pakistan[c]	$3.64 billion drop 880,000 impacted	Potential loss to GDP from travel and tourism earnings (June 2020) Jobs at risk
Sri Lanka[c]	$1.99 billion drop 200,000 impacted	Potential loss to GDP from travel and tourism earnings (June 2020) Jobs at risk
Fiji[d]	84.8% drop in 2020 vs 2019	Decline in international tourism revenue (March 2021)
Cambodia[e]	> 90% of registered and nonregistered MSMEs	Reduction in sales since lockdown, the majority lost over 50% (October 2020)
Thailand, Sri Lanka, Viet Nam, Cambodia, Nepal[f]	80% drop	Estimated loss of revenue from tourism activity (November 2020)
CAREC countries[g]	1 million jobs at risk	Due to loss in aviation activity, estimated loss of jobs (February 2021)

CAREC = Central Asia Regional Economic Cooperation; FY = fiscal year; GDP = gross domestic product; MICE = meetings, incentives, conferences, and exhibitions; MSME = micro, small, and medium enterprises.

[a] International Monetary Fund. *Samoa: Request for Disbursement Under the Rapid Credit Facility-Press Release; Staff Report; and Statement by the Executive Director for Samoa.*

[b] MFAT and SPTO. 2020. *Pacific Tourism: Covid 19 Impact and Recovery. Sector Status Report: Phase 1B.*

[c] L. Twining Ward and J. F. McComb. 2020. *COVID-19 and Tourism in South Asia: Opportunities for Sustainable Regional Outcomes.* Washington, DC: World Bank.

[d] Fiji Bureau of Statistics. 2021. Fiji's Earnings from Tourism-December Quarter and Annual 2020. *FBoS Release No: 07, 2021.*

[e] The Asia Foundation. *Enduring the Pandemic: Rapid Survey in the Impact of COVID-19 on MSMEs in the Tourism Sector and Households in Cambodia.*

[f] PATA. 2020. *COVID-19 and The Tourism Sector: A Comparison of Policy Response in Asia Pacific.*

[g] ADB. 2021. *Impact of COVID-19 on CAREC Aviation and Tourism.* Manila.

Source: Authors' compilation.

Box 13: Economic Impacts of Reduced Aviation in Central Asia

There are 25 airlines based in the Central Asia Regional Economic Cooperation (CAREC) zone, and with a few exceptions, they rely on the international markets for revenue. In September 2020, international passenger numbers to, from, and within CAREC were 90% lower compared with prepandemic levels. As a result, in 2020 CAREC experienced 40 million fewer passengers, leading to an estimated loss of $7 billion in revenue and 1 million jobs. The impact on gross domestic product in CAREC countries is estimated to be a $27 billion drop. For airlines to survive, support of $2 billion may be needed.

A focus on domestic or regional travel is challenging given that only 3% of total CAREC traffic is interregional and only 27% of traffic is domestic, leaving a 70% international travel gap that needs to be compensated for. Kazakhstan and Pakistan have large domestic markets and internal travel has recovered well. In contrast, Georgia—the country most dependent on international arrivals—has not seen much recovery. Impacts of tourism halts on sustainable development have not been assessed.

Sources: ADB and Central Asia Regional Economic Cooperation. 2021. *Impact of COVID-19 On CAREC Aviation and Tourism*. Manila; and ADB. 2021. ADB, EIB Join Forces to Protect Oceans, Support the Blue Economy. News release. 15 January.

Differentiated Impacts

The impacts of COVID-19 vary across tourism industries and destinations. Impact factors of COVID-19 include the wider-than-tourism response to the pandemic, health situations, preparedness and resilience, and crisis governance. Moreover, countries with access to domestic tourism markets have experienced busy periods. In some destinations, the number of guest nights has increased compared to previous years, while others have seen guest nights reach close to zero. Guest-night data is available in most countries. Figure 10 illustrates COVID-19 impacts by subsector, such as accommodation and travel (Yang et al. 2020). The index shows recovery (change to prepandemic levels) since the main impact of the pandemic in mid-March 2020. Local mobility data indicates that people are moving more locally, possibly benefitting industries such as restaurants and retail outlets.

Accommodation industry. Data from December 2020 suggests that most properties in the accommodation industry across Asia and the Pacific had reopened, but that occupancy rates remained low. The PRC outperformed most peers, with 49% of rooms occupied, while other Asian countries saw occupancy rates closer to 38%, with some of the lowest rates observed in India, Japan, Thailand, and Viet Nam. Oceania performed at 45%, with both Australia and New Zealand achieving higher results than the Pacific island countries. One of the key performance measures for hotels is the revenue per room generated. This indicator has dropped significantly in all regions, for example by 59% across all open hotels in Asia (excluding the PRC), and by 47% in Australia and Oceania.

Airport and cruise industries. Industry-specific data for airports shows considerable negative pandemic impacts, with a $111.8 billion loss in 2020 revenue against business-as-usual projections (ICAO 2021). The cruise industry also reported significant revenue losses in 2020, in the order of 99.5%. The Carnival Corporation alone experienced a decrease in revenue from $6.5 billion in 2019 to $31 million in 2020 (Hiltner and Fisher 2021).

Arts and culture. In the first wave of the crisis, 90% of countries closed their World Heritage sites, and about 85,000 museums closed. In November 2020, UNESCO reported that World Heritage sites in 26% of countries were temporarily closed entirely, sites in 44% of countries had reopened, and 30% were partially opened (UNESCO 2020). Reduced revenue is leading to the deterioration of sites and/or closures. Reduced revenue to heritage sites has the potential to unevenly affect some communities or groups, for example, indigenous people.

Figure 10: Global COVID-19 Tourism Index and Subindexes

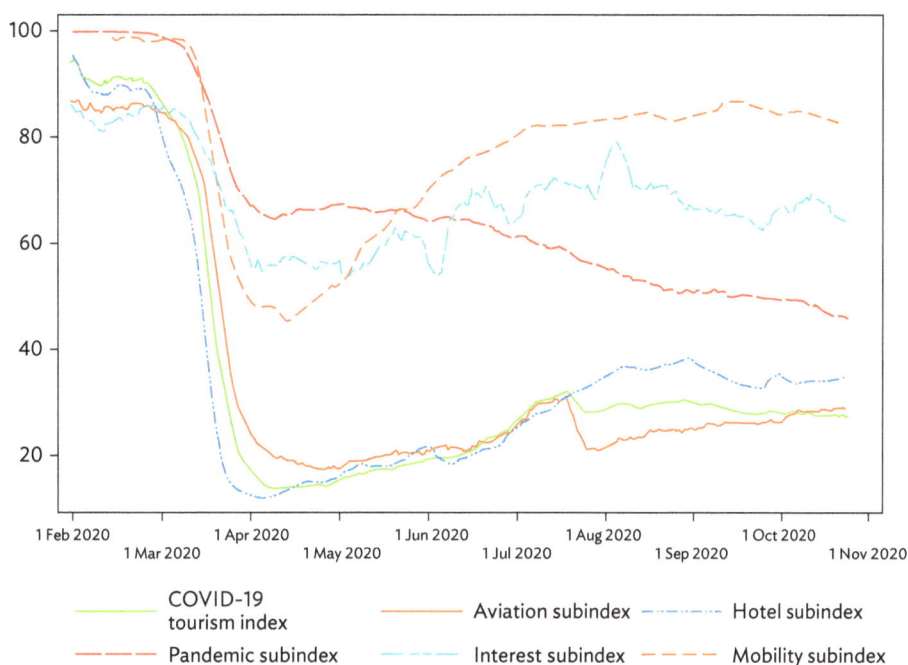

Source: Y. Yang et al. 2020. Monitoring the Global COVID-19 Impact on Tourism: The COVID-19 Tourism Index. *Annals of Tourism.*

Based on data collected in 14 countries, the International Labour Organization (ILO) has indicated the jobs and livelihoods of at least 15.3 million tourism workers are at risk (ILO 2020). Risks include taking unpaid leave, accepting lower wages, or losing employment. Tourism workers are particularly at risk if they rely on informal tourism jobs (Chapter 4.1). Employment risks can have extensive detrimental effects on livelihoods, as in many cases, one tourism job supports multiple family members.

In Maldives, the Ministry of Economic Development undertook a Rapid COVID-19 Livelihoods Assessment and found that 45,000 resort employees (of which 22,000 are Maldivians) are directly affected by the pandemic. Young employees (with less than 2 years of employment) and males were more affected. The assessment revealed that 16% of employees lost jobs, while the remaining 84% retained them with either reduced or no pay (ADB 2020).

Business Responses

The economic impacts from reduced tourism continue to evolve, and business planning is hampered by changing health conditions and government policies. Businesses face extreme uncertainty with tourism flows, increased costs due to hygiene protocols, and wider economic fluctuations. Depending on location, type, and scale, tourism businesses have experienced the following:

(i)   suspended or reduced service for certain periods to reduce losses;
(ii)   reduced staff numbers (temporarily or permanently);
(iii)   temporarily shut down operations to minimize costs, while staying ready to reopen;

(iv)   reduced business costs, including high commissions paid to intermediaries (such as online booking engines) by encouraging direct bookings;

(v)   adapted products to meet the needs of local or domestic visitors;

(vi)   redefined the company, its purpose, or its business model;

(vii)   used the opportunity to undertake maintenance, training, or reposition the company;

(viii) restructured operational activities by moving meetings online, including for staff, suppliers, collaborators, and distribution channels; and

(ix)   retrained and/or lent staff to other businesses in higher demand.

A survey of MSMEs in Cambodia showed that in October 2020, 55% of businesses considered themselves at high risk of business failure. The risk for registered businesses was perceived to be higher than for nonregistered ones (The Asia Foundation 2021). The expected length of survival depended on the business type, with travel agents and hotels displaying the greatest risk of failure (Figure 11). The reason is their disproportional dependence on international travel.

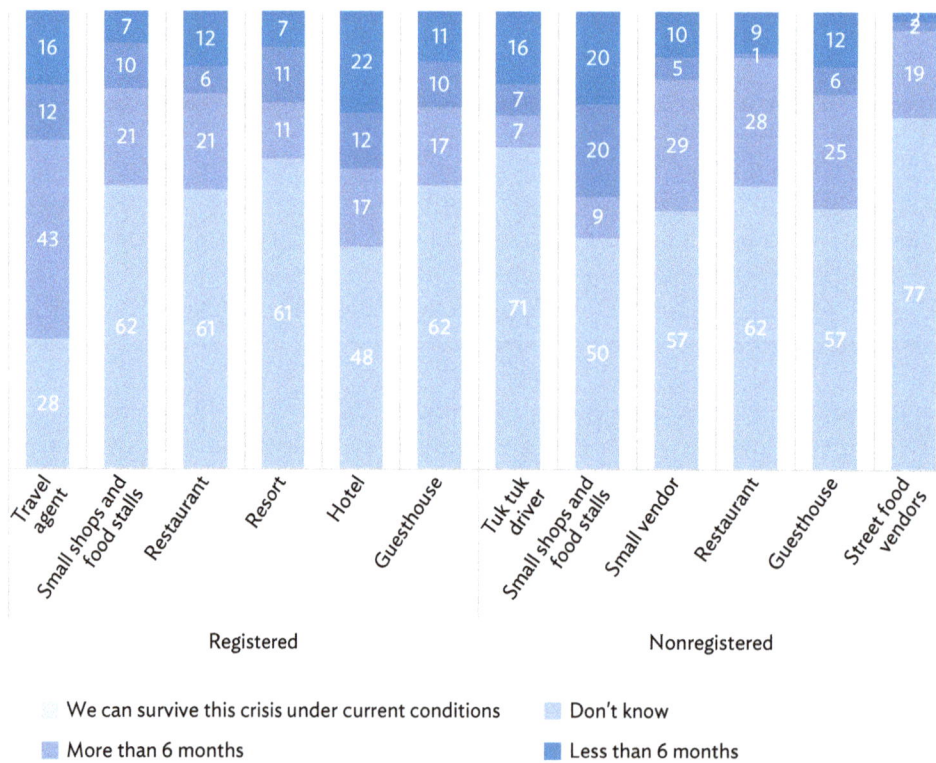

Figure 11: Perceived Timeframe of Potential Business Failure Among Small and Medium-Sized Enterprises in Cambodia (%)

Note: A *tuk tuk* is a three-wheeled motorized vehicle used as a taxi in Cambodia.
Source: The Asia Foundation. 2021. Enduring the Pandemic: Rapid Survey in the Impact of COVID-19 on MSMEs in the Tourism Sector and Households in Cambodia.

Box 14: Digitalizing Services—The Uptake of Virtual Tourism

In response to lockdowns, many destinations and operators have made virtual tourism experiences available. These range from climbing Mount Everest, to visiting Angkor Wat, and online tours of Tokyo. In Indonesia, the Ministry for Tourism and Creative Economy organized several virtual tourism events, including the Geotourism Festival 2020. Traveloka—the largest travel portal in Indonesia—is now offering virtual tourism experiences for a range of destinations.

The potential for—and positive impacts of—virtual tourism are mixed. While destinations, tour operators, and event organizers may keep a presence—and even raise some revenue—local and often smaller businesses miss out. One key benefit of digitized travel is reductions in carbon footprints from travel.

Source: M. M. Aminy. 2020. Can Virtual Tourism Save Local Businesses in Tourist Destinations? *The Conversation.* 2 December.

Environmental Changes

Reduced economic activity—including tourism—drove the largest annual reduction in CO_2 emissions since World War II (Le Quéré et al. 2020). The drop equated to 2.4 billion tons of carbon—or 7%—which is in line with the amount needed to reduce emissions each year from 2020 to 2030 to remain within the 1.5°C international carbon budget. The long-term effects of COVID-19 on the environment will depend largely on how "green" recovery is, and whether government support packages and enabling factors address the environmental challenges of tourism (Hepburn et al. 2020).

The impact of reduced travel on the environment is multilayered (Table 4). For example, to understand how animals might reclaim space, the Wildlife Institute of India launched the citizen science platform "Lockdown Wildlife Tracker." Data from around the world highlights how wildlife moves into areas normally dominated by people. Conversely, however, evidence suggests that loss of tourism revenue severely undermines conservation activities (Lindsey et al. 2020).

For some, the pandemic has heightened awareness of environmental issues. Research published in January 2021 notes that 76% of consumers were more concerned about sustainability after COVID-19 (Earth Changers 2021). When asked about "sustainable tourism", 14% more consumers were concerned with sustainability after the pandemic than before.

Research published in 2020 also signals an increased desire to explore places closer to home, reconnect with nature, and travel "off-the-beaten-path" through outdoor and nonurban activities. This may provide an important opportunity to stimulate further environmental awareness (WTTC 2020). While there might be an increased interest in ecotourism activities, one expert interviewee warned that certain types of wildlife tourism encounters require careful management to partly minimize the risk of further transmission of viruses from animals to humans.

Table 4: Environmental Impacts of COVID-19-Induced Reductions in Tourism

Parameter	Observed Impact
Greenhouse gas emissions[a]	Daily global CO_2 emissions decreased by 17% by early April 2020 compared with the mean 2019 levels; aviation CO_2 emissions declined by 60%.
Waste management[b,c]	The need for greater hygiene has increased waste. Excessive use of hand sanitizer is detrimental to human health and the environment.
Water consumption[d]	Two effects were observed so far. One is a decrease in water consumption due to reduced economic activity. On the other hand, increased water consumption was recorded due to frequent hand washing and deep cleaning. Hygiene measures also harm water quality due to the use of toxic substances.
Wildlife conservation and ecosystems[e,c,f]	While some areas have recovered due to reduced disturbance from tourism, there is increasing concern that the loss of nature tourism puts protected areas and biodiversity conservation efforts at risk.
Air quality[g]	Air quality, especially in urban areas, has improved considerably during periods of lockdown, but impacts differ across pollutants.
General interest in sustainability[h]	The pandemic has accelerated the need to implement policies for sustainable development, although this could be hampered by increased economic pressure. For example, the Cook Islands sees a rollback on environmental protection as plans advance to develop mining, justified as a diversification strategy away from tourism.

[a] C. Le Qur et al. 2020. Temporary Reduction in Daily Global CO2 Emissions During the COVID-19 Forced Confinement. *Nature Climate Change*. 10 (7). pp. 647–653.
[b] A. Mahmood et al. 2020. COVID-19 and Frequent Use of Hand Sanitizers; Human Health and Environmental Hazards by Exposure Pathways. *Science of the Total Environment*. 742(140561).
[c] P. F. Rupani et al. 2020. Coronavirus Pandemic (COVID-19) and Its Natural Environmental Impacts. International *Journal of Environmental Science and Technology*. September (1). pp. 1–12.
[d] J. Quintua and D. Marcelo. 2020. Estimated Impact of COVID-19 on Water Needs and Volume and Quality of Wastewater.
[e] P. Lindsey et al. 2020. Conserving Africa's Wildlife and Wildlands through the COVID-19 Crisis and Beyond. *Nature Ecology and Evolution*. 4. pp. 1300–1310.
[f] J. Waithaka et al. 2021. Impacts of COVID-19 on Protected and Conserved Areas: A Global Overview and Regional Perspectives. *Parks*. 27. pp. 41–56.
[g] M. Ghahremanloo et al. 2021. Impact of the COVID-19 Outbreak on Air Pollution Levels in East Asia. *Science of The Total Environment*. 754 (42226).
[h] R. Golden Kroner et al. 2021. COVID-Era Policies and Economic Recovery Plans: Are Governments Building Back Better for Protected and Conserved Areas? *Parks*. 27. pp. 135–148.
Source: Authors' compilation.

Box 15: Tourism Revenue and its Impacts on Wildlife Conservation

Cardamom Tented Camp is a three-way initiative that grew from the need for a sustainable tourism development project to obtain an Eco-Tourism, Eco Lodge and Conservation Concession by the Royal Government of Cambodia. The eco lodge camp opened in 2017 in Botum Sakor national park in southwest Cambodia. A percentage of tourism revenue goes to the Wildlife Alliance and any additional profits are reinvested locally.

The pandemic-related closure of Cardamom Tented Camp in Cambodia led to the suspension of forest patrols by Wildlife Alliance rangers. The rangers' equipment, food, and wages are funded through tourism. Before COVID-19, illegal hunting in the National Park had declined by 90%, but there is a risk that poaching will increase again. In the meantime, the foundation has launched an emergency page on the crowdfunding platform FundRazr. Cardamom Tented Camp will offer donors who give over $200 a free night on top of a 2-night-stay, once borders open again.

Source: J. Louie. 2020. *Wildlife Conservation in Cambodia is Being Hit Hard by Covid-19. Here's How You Can Help.* DestinAsia.

Policy Responses

Global and regional organizations relevant to tourism have coordinated responses through a range of initiatives. Most measures focus on immediate crisis response rather than long-term planning to increase the contribution of tourism to the SDGs. The Association of Southeast Asian Nations (ASEAN) tourism ministers, for example, issued a joint statement to expedite information exchange through enhanced cooperation of the ASEAN Tourism Crisis Communication Team. A post-COVID-19 crisis recovery plan aims to advance ASEAN as a unified destination and to develop micro and macroeconomic policies for MSME recovery. A Travel Corridor Arrangement Task Force has been established to facilitate intraregional travel. Also focusing on enabling travel during or postpandemic, the tourism ministers of the G20 produced the G20 Guidelines for Action on Safe and Seamless Travel.

Types of Policy Responses

According to the OECD (2020), the pandemic has triggered three key types of national policy:

(i)   business support programs, including loans or nationalization of strategically important firms (like airlines);
(ii)   sectoral schemes targeted at tourism to support crisis committees, training and capacity building programs, or sectors workforce support programs; and
(iii) untargeted support schemes providing liquidity to firms and job-retention schemes.

The measures put in place reflect different timeframes at which response outcomes are targeted, namely making it through the crisis, adapting to the new normal, and cultivating resilience (Twining Ward and McComb 2020, WTTC 2020). While this report does not focus on the third category, which is of most interest in embedding sustainability into tourism, tourism has benefitted substantially from untargeted measures. Unfortunately, relatively little thought has been given to strategic changes in tourism, as governments balance immediate needs with long-term opportunities. UNWTO maintains an online portal with information on government support measures (Figure 12).

There is a wide range of measures that focus on securing health and safety and providing either fiscal or monetary support. Almost 90% of countries analyzed implemented economic stimulus measures, and more than half of all countries provided financial support to the sector (Barkas et al. 2020). While short-term financial injections are critical for successful crisis response, they are not sustainable in the long term and present the risk of prolonging inevitable bankruptcies.

Fiscal policies such as wage subsidies and tax breaks are costly, especially for developing countries, and those with limited funds have put a limit of 3 to 6 months on those initiatives, indicating expectations of recovery timeframes. The financial tradeoff of business support packages is becoming visible as governments are cutting funds elsewhere.

Some countries developed policy measures for specific tourism businesses, including support for airlines (OECD 2020). As of August 2020, governments in 52 countries had provided financial support to airlines, totaling about $160 billion. Two thirds of the funds were provided as direct aid (subsidies, loans, equity, or cash), while one third covered wage subsidies. Some studies note that government support packages have favored national carriers that had become "too big to fail" (Abate et al. 2020). Very few countries have attached environmental conditionality to bailouts (UN 2020).

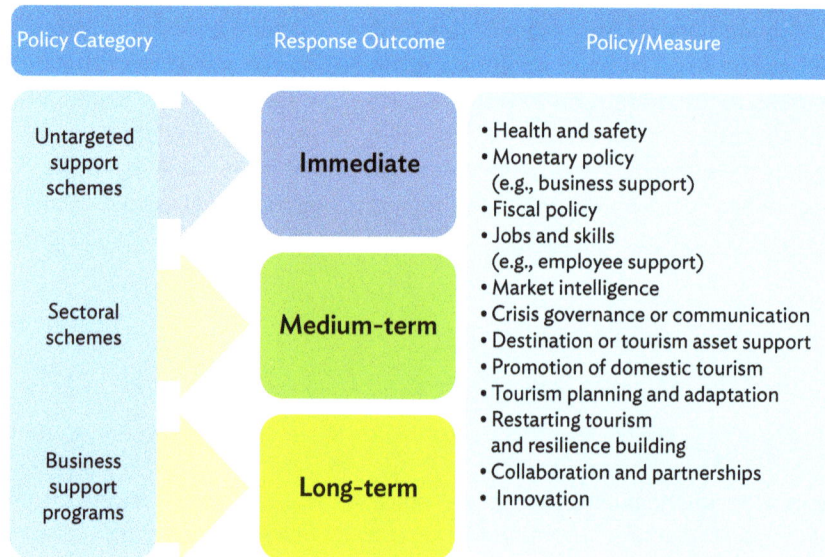

Figure 12: Tourism Policy Response Framework

Policy Category	Response Outcome	Policy/Measure
Untargeted support schemes	**Immediate**	• Health and safety • Monetary policy (e.g., business support) • Fiscal policy • Jobs and skills (e.g., employee support)
Sectoral schemes	**Medium-term**	• Market intelligence • Crisis governance or communication • Destination or tourism asset support • Promotion of domestic tourism • Tourism planning and adaptation
Business support programs	**Long-term**	• Restarting tourism and resilience building • Collaboration and partnerships • Innovation

Source: Authors' compilation based on UNWTO. 2021. *COVID-19: Measures to Support Travel and Tourism.*

Medium- and longer-term policy responses include skill and capacity building programs, including retraining workers to find employment in different industries (Table 5) (Barkas et al. 2020). Several governments have also invested in shifting from international to domestic tourism, repositioning destinations, and investing in assets. Few policies have taken a long-term focus, such as including sustainability criteria in financial support packages, extending social protection, and redesigning tourism systems (UN 2020).

Table 5: Policy Measures Targeting Medium- or Long-Term Tourism Recovery

Existing Policy Measures to Address Medium- or Long-Term Recovery and Change	Policy Category	Example
Retraining and upskilling programs for laid-off workers (making short courses delivered by the Ministry of Tourism mandatory for workers to receive government support)[a]	Jobs and skills	Cambodia
Education scheme to improve skills, incentives to retain workforce, and training or mentoring programs[b,c]	Jobs and skills	Bhutan, Cook Islands, Malaysia, Thailand
Retraining tourism workers to support the health sector[d]	Jobs and skills	Bangladesh, Nepal
Financial support for building and renovating attractions in local communities[e]	Monetary; Restarting tourism	Thailand
Simplify hotel classification system, legitimizing sharing economy accommodation platforms, and relaxing regulations for the camping industry[e]	Restarting tourism	Republic of Korea
Green recovery measures (e.g., clean up campaigns)[c]	Restarting tourism	Cambodia

continued

Table 5: *continued*

Existing Policy Measures to Address Medium- or Long-Term Recovery and Change	Policy Category	Example
Monitoring tourism industry data; research on impact and recovery[d,f]	Market intelligence	Australia, Nepal, New Zealand Pakistan, Singapore,
Using domestic tourism as a recovery vehicle[c,d]	Domestic tourism; Tourism planning	Bhutan, Sri Lanka, Viet Nam, Thailand
Planning for recovery, for instance, conducting a study to "reimagine" tourism post COVID-19[e]	Tourism planning; Innovation	New Zealand
The ADB impact investment platform, ADB Ventures, has teamed up with the Tourism Authority of Thailand to support technology start-ups with the "TakeMeTour" to develop the LocalFarm online platform and help mitigate pandemic impacts on the tourism sector of Thailand[f]	Innovation; Restarting tourism	Thailand
Tourism Crises Response and Recovery Plan (TCRRP) supported by the Vanuatu Sustainable Tourism Strategy (VSTS) (2021–2025). The focus of the strategy is to enable a transition of the tourism industry to become more resilient[g,h]	Tourism planning	Vanuatu

[a] United Nations. 2020. *Policy Brief: COVID-19 and Transforming Tourism*. New York: United Nations.
[b] International Labour Organization. *COVID-19 and Employment in the Tourism Sector: Impact and Response in Asia and the Pacific*.
[c] PATA. 2020. *COVID-19 and the Tourism Sector: A Comparison of Policy Response in Asia Pacific*.
[d] L. Twining Ward and J. F. McComb. 2020. *COVID-19 and Tourism in South Asia: Opportunities for Sustainable Regional Outcomes*. Washington, DC: World Bank.
[e] WTTC. 2020. *To Recovery and Beyond: The Future of Travel and Tourism in the Wake of COVID-19*.
[f] UNWTO. 2021. *COVID-19: Measures to Support Travel and Tourism*.
[g] Government of Vanuatu, Department of Tourism. 2020. *Phase 1: Response. Immediate Safety, Response and Economic Recovery Effort*.
[h] Government of Vanuatu, Department of Tourism. 2021. *Vanuatu Sustainable Tourism Strategy 2021–2025*.
Source: Authors' compilation.

Box 16: Recovery Plans in the Philippines

The Philippines' Department of Tourism developed a Tourism Response and Recovery Plan in consultation with the Tourism Congress, an organization comprising representatives from all accredited tourism enterprises and other stakeholders in the industry. This is the government master plan for tourism recovery. It aims to protect and ensure employment and business survival, enable the government and private sector to work toward a sustainable and resilient tourism industry for the future, and provide policies and guidelines for a "new normal."

The Philippines' Department of Tourism is also launching a Sustainable Tourism Development Project, an initiative under Transforming Communities Toward Resilient, Inclusive, and Sustainable Tourism. The project is a collaboration between the Philippines' Department of Tourism, the provincial government of Palawan, the municipalities of Coron and El Nido, and ADB. The 5-year project focuses on urban infrastructure, ecosystem improvement, and enterprise development for a more sustainable and inclusive tourism sector.

Source: Government of the Philippines, Department of Tourism. 2020. *Guidelines in Handling Guests in Tourism Enterprises in the Advent of nCOV Global Health Emergency*. Manila.

4 Expert Insights

This chapter provides expert insights into three areas that deserve close attention. It looks at the impact on women working in tourism, the impact of the pandemic on the Pacific, and plans for the transformation of tourism in Thailand. Women in tourism have been particularly impacted by the pandemic and the response to this will have implications for social inclusion. Pacific island countries have several highly tourism-dependent economies with limited opportunities for domestic tourism compared to many others in Asia and the Pacific. Nevertheless, the region holds important lessons on the role of regional cooperation on tourism and embracing a transformative mindset on sustainable tourism. Thailand is a regional tourism powerhouse. Its response to the impact of the pandemic and emerging opportunities for the transformation of tourism in Thailand holds important lessons for many.

The chapter highlights best practices and emerging opportunities to support the development of a more sustainable tourism industry as travel resumes.

Impact of COVID-19 on Women in Tourism

Prepared by Elaine Chiao Ling Yang, Griffith University

Women in tourism have been particularly impacted by the pandemic because of the gendered nature of tourism work and other underlying social barriers to the employment of women. Below is a brief analysis of the impact and current pandemic response programs, followed by a discussion of opportunities to address gender inequality.

Gendered Tourism Work and Entrepreneurship

Women are disproportionately affected by pandemic-induced unemployment due to gender segregation in hard-hit sectors, and because they are overrepresented in casual and front-facing employment (Chapter 2.2) (Workplace Gender Equality Agency 2020). Care responsibilities further undermine labor force participation, as more women take up casual employment than men (McKinsey & Company 2020).

Casual workers are bearing the heaviest burden during the pandemic and are less protected by social security, including sick leave entitlements and income replacement during lockdowns. Those who remain employed in a front-line service role are exposed to the risk of contracting the virus, as hospitality venues have a heightened risk of COVID-19 infection (Chang et al. 2021).

The gendered nature of work across industries accounts for a quarter of the gender difference of pandemic-induced unemployment, while systemic social barriers explain the rest (McKinsey & Company 2020). The closure of schools and daycare centers has put additional strains on women doing unpaid domestic and care work. Juggling between paid and unpaid work hinders the participation of women in and reentry into the labor force. The traditional belief that women should be the primary caretakers has impacted decisions taken within households and organizations more broadly about who gets to keep their jobs. This is especially pertinent in Asian countries where men often have greater access to jobs than women.

Pandemic impacts are amplified for women in informal economies, which include the accommodation, food services, and souvenir categories (ILO 2020). Women constitute 90% of sellers and producers in ethnic minority souvenir businesses, and the halt of tourism has led many female souvenir vendors to lose their livelihoods (Trupp and Sunanta 2017). Often, informal workers are excluded from most government aid packages and have limited access to social and legal protection, which has rendered them some of the most vulnerable groups during the crisis.

Women tourism entrepreneurs—in both the formal and informal economy—belong to another pandemic-stricken group. Women have less access to financial services and loans than men (OECD 2016). As a result, women-owned tourism businesses—especially those in the informal economy—are usually smaller and have limited capital to withstand the pandemic and are at heightened risk as economies contract (United Nations Conference on Trade and Development 2020).

Many countries in Asia and the Pacific offer COVID-19 aid to MSMEs (ILO 2020). However, it is unclear to what extent women-owned businesses have benefited. Social barriers such as the digital gender gap may hinder the reach of these packages to women, while psychological barriers and experiences with unsuccessful financing applications could deter the uptake of loan programs by women (McKinsey & Company 2020, OECD 2016). Without targeted policies, women entrepreneurs in tourism may face greater challenges in sustaining their business than men.

Migrant Female Tourism Workers

Tourism is a main source of jobs for migrants because hospitality jobs have low skill requirements and low barriers to entry. At the same time, migrant workers are essential to meet labor market shortages, filling jobs unwanted by locals. There are an estimated 20 million migrant workers in Southeast Asia and the actual number is higher if expanded to include undocumented migrant workers (UN Myanmar 2020). Among migrant workers, one third are women, and many work in hospitality. The travel hiatus has reduced the demand for migrant hospitality workers.

Many migrant workers are stranded without employment or income support. As jobs slowly return with the easing of lockdowns, migrant workers are exposed to a higher risk of virus contraction and community outbreaks due to their living conditions (Koh 2020, Vendergeest et al. 2021). Further, migrant workers with insecure employment are more likely to work multiple jobs to survive and less likely to take leave despite having minor symptoms. Undocumented migrants are reluctant to get tested because of their illegal status while migrant workers who manage—or are forced to—return home suffer unemployment and income insecurity (Wongsamuth 2021, ILO 2020).

Migrant female workers—especially those with undocumented status and those who work in the informal sectors (including sex tourism)—are susceptible to precarious employment and exploitation in normal times, which renders them particularly vulnerable during crises (Baum et al. 2020). Evidence suggests that undocumented female migrant workers are at risk of modern slavery, trafficking, and gendered violence at the hands of traffickers or intimate partners (Global Policy Journal 2020, Phromkade 2020).

Box 17: Soaring Domestic Violence in Asia and the Pacific

In addition to financial hardship resulting from business closures and growing unemployment, women are experiencing an alarming rate of domestic violence associated with the pandemic. In Singapore, the number of calls to domestic violence helplines increased by 137% just 2 months into the lockdown. A similar trend has been reported in Jakarta, Indonesia, with domestic violence cases tripling just 2 weeks after the lockdown measures were imposed.[a]

Home confinement due to lockdowns and unemployment has left women more vulnerable than ever to abusive partners. The pandemic-induced personal crises, psychological stress, and financial setbacks could trigger the abusers and intensify the violence.[b] The disruption of social networks and support services during health crises means victims are left with little support in the face of intensified violence.[c]

[a] T. I. Oktavianti. 2020. Jakarta Records Spike in Domestic Violence Reports During Work-From-Home Period. *The Jakarta Post.*
[b] A. Taub. 2020. A New Covid-19 Crisis: Domestic Abuse Rises Worldwide. *The New York Times.*
[c] The Asia Foundation. 2021. *Enduring the Pandemic: Rapid Survey in the Impact of COVID-19 on MSMEs in the Tourism Sector and Households in Cambodia.*
Source: Adapted from Association of Women for Action and Research. COVID-19 and the Increase of Domestic Violence Against Women. Geneva: Office of the United Nations High Commissioner for Human Rights.

Responses and Opportunities to Address Gender Issues

Many countries in the Asia and Pacific region have introduced fiscal packages, tax relief, and loans targeting the tourism sector (Chapter 3.3). However, few countries offer gender-responsive measures.

Nongovernment organizations such as UN Women and UNWTO advocate for an explicit gender component in national and business response and recovery strategies. The two agencies have worked together and developed guidelines for inclusive recovery, one of which focuses on women in tourism (UNWTO 2021). Nonetheless, little evidence suggests their uptake and implementation.

The pandemic has raised critical issues about gender inequalities. The tourism sector has empowered women by providing work and a livelihood that would otherwise not be available to them. However, the framing of gender equality in tourism has so far focused on economic empowerment without proper emphasis on broader social and structural inequalities that have disadvantaged women in tourism, as revealed by the pandemic.

Countries and businesses are now transitioning from crisis to recovery planning, and this transition offers an opportunity to embed and mainstream gender equality into recovery road maps, to rebuild in a fairer way. The following five themes can encourage a gender-sensitive and responsive recovery.

(i)   **Industry-specific gender disaggregated data.** The UN recommends a gender component in all national pandemic assessments to investigate and address the impact of COVID-19 on women. Existing gender disaggregated data focuses on the direct impact of COVID-19 such as infection and mortality rates. Gender disaggregated data on secondary impacts—encompassing the economic, social, and health (including psychological health and gender-based violence)—should inform inclusive recovery policies. These secondary effects are likely to endure for years after the pandemic and require longer-term strategies. However, data on women in tourism is scarce.

(ii) **Mainstreaming gender in COVID-19 response and recovery measures.** Countries and tourism businesses need to mainstream gender by explicitly including a gender component in their COVID-19 response and recovery measures to address gender gaps. One integral step is to include the voices of women in recovery road maps, which also presents opportunities for women to access leadership and decision-making positions in the region, where women are underrepresented. Further, the implementation and outcomes of gender-responsive measures need to be monitored to ensure benefits reach targeted recipients, especially among the most disadvantaged groups.

(iii) **Intersectional approach to gender-responsive measures.** Gender-responsive measures should consider interlocking social inequalities. Flexible and remote work arrangements may reduce barriers for women in tourism at managerial positions and in professional spheres. This arrangement is impractical for many women in tourism who are employed in low-level manual jobs, which require physical presence at the workplace. Similarly, informal and migrant female workers in tourism face entirely different pandemic-induced hardships. For gender-responsive measures to be effective, an understanding of the intersecting forms of vulnerability—such as from gender, class, race, and migrant status—is necessary to devise differentiated measures for different groups of women. Without a nuanced understanding of the complex social mechanisms that contribute to gender disparities, the measures will have limited effectiveness.

(iv) **Regional collaboration to address migrant workers' rights.** Regional collaboration among countries in Asia and the Pacific is imperative to address issues that have arisen from intraregional labor migration. These include extending unemployment benefits and health care to migrant workers remaining in host countries; providing safe passages and quarantine facilities for migrant workers returning home; and terminating pandemic-induced human trafficking and exploitation.

Instead of penalizing undocumented migrant workers in informal economies, these measures should foster safe migration and provide incentives for businesses to register their workers. A gender-sensitive approach is also needed to address female migrant workers' vulnerability to exploitation and gendered violence. The labor rights and safety of migrant workers need to be at the forefront of recovery plans when demand for migrant workers resurges.

(v) **Opportunities for upskilling and reskilling.** The temporary standstill in tourism presents an opportunity for governments and tourism businesses to invest in capacity building to get ready for when travel resumes. Upskilling programs for female tourism workers address the concentration of women in lower level jobs. Reskilling programs are much needed, considering pandemic-induced job transitions manifested in the wide adoption of digitization (McKinsey & Company 2020). Digital competency training will benefit women entrepreneurs in tourism by helping them (a) navigate digital distribution channels; (b) showcase their services and products such as crafts, guest houses, and tours online; (c) access government recovery packages and credit from financial institutions; and (d) register their businesses. Financial assistance for women to invest in digital devices and for developing countries to expand digital infrastructure in rural areas will be fruitful. Likewise, returning migrant women can benefit from government-funded reskilling programs to transfer skills gained from migrant work to help rebuild tourism sectors in home provinces and countries.

Advancing gender equality in tourism would result in benefits from productive workforce participation, improve business performance, and contribute to inclusive societies and economies so they can become more resilient to future crises.

Impact of COVID-19 on the Pacific

Prepared by Apisalome Movono, Massey University, New Zealand

In 2019, tourism provided over $1.5 billion to South Pacific Tourism Organization (SPTO) member countries while employing over 5 million people either directly or indirectly. The near collapse of the tourism system has revealed its vulnerability to shocks. However, the pandemic has also spurred Pacific people to respond positively, showing signs of resilience.

This section focuses on opportunities that arise from Pacific people's responses to the pandemic using insights from research conducted on affected tourism-based communities and online interviews with leading tourism officials to inform this report.

Impact on Pacific Island Communities

Tourism-dependent communities in the Pacific suffered significant financial difficulties due to the loss of tourism-based income: 73% of those completing a survey in mid-2020 said they had experienced a "major decline" in household income and 60% of respondents were from households that relied on tourism for half of the total household revenue (Scheyvens and Movono 2020). The sudden effect of the global lockdown and lack of international guests spurred a domino effect impacting handicraft and other tourism-related MSMEs. Some tourism operators had to close, reassign staff, or put employees on reduced hours. In contrast, some operators took a people-centered approach, providing financial and social support to workers.

Research indicates a rise in people turning to loan sharks, increased petty theft, alcoholism, violence, family disruptions, and inability to repay debts after investing in tourism assets. This created feelings of "despair" and "hopelessness" for some. Financial well-being declined considerably, but other findings were more mixed. In some instances, people reported mental well-being improvements resulting from adapting to the pandemic.

Pacific communities sought support from both traditional and alternative sources when tourism stalled, leading many to leave tourist towns and return to their villages. Fortunately, many were part of communities that place immense value on kinship systems, traditional indigenous knowledge, and customary land and resources. People utilized their available social, ecological, and cultural resources to cope with COVID-19 and other vulnerabilities. Cultural systems that enforce peoples' custodianship of resources and society become a platform from which sustenance and resilience are maintained (Movono et al. 2018).

People used several economic strategies for survival—including growing their food—and in some cases, resumed bartering. Many households sold or gifted surplus produce as a matter of necessity and based on goodwill. Some started small businesses, including women who had previously been resort employees starting events and catering businesses.

Studies demonstrate that the pandemic forced people to reconnect with their ancestral land and various livelihoods practices that have helped improve food security (Vunibola and Leweniqila 2020, Farrell et al. 2020). People reportedly began to plant more volume and variety of crops and vegetables conducive to health and well-being. Researchers in the Pacific also highlighted that "No one is going hungry," because (a) people had access to customary land on which to grow food; and (b) customary systems meant that neighbors, clan members, and church communities helped to provide for those who were more vulnerable. Communities retained sufficient knowledge to teach younger members who had lost jobs about growing food and fishing.

Opportunities for Recovery

(i) **Respecting the strengths and resilience of traditional ways.** People in the Pacific are relearning and reinvigorating indigenous knowledge, diversifying their skill sets, and sustaining life. These bonds were explicitly observed in Vatuolalai, a Fijian village situated next to an all-inclusive resort, to enforce indigenous philosophies such as *solesolevaki* (or communal solidarity) structurally. These themes of collective strength guided behavior and maintained solidarity within communities during COVID-19 (Movono and Scheyvens 2020, Movono 2017).

Traditional governance structures, such as the Vanuatu chiefly system, Fiji Matanitu Vanua system, Matai system, and other Pacific equivalents, have primarily championed indigenous issues. These structures are holistic and have circular features that sustain the livelihoods and well-being of Pacific people. These governance systems connect to and hold ownership of over 80% of land resources in the Pacific. Resource custodianships use patterns—such as those in Vanuatu—operate within the local culture, supporting livelihoods systems that are diverse and resilient in the face of future perturbations, including climate change. Responses to shocks and resilience-building must extend beyond current sustainable development boundaries, acknowledge indigeneity, and include local culture and practices as part of future tourism considerations.

(ii) **Recognizing and supporting tourism workers: complementing the Pacific way of life.** Pacific tourism employees—although having mixed feelings—want tourism to return. However, they desire better wages, job security, insurance for shocks, and better working conditions. While some suggested reducing tourist numbers in crowded areas, others urged governments to promote off-season tourism, open new locations to avoid crowding, and spread the economic benefits more widely. People in landowning communities would also like greater local ownership and control of tourism enterprises—including joint ventures—building on existing strengths such as cultural or tropical garden tours and agritourism.

People who would like to earn cash while also engaging in community development also mentioned flexible hours and part-time work. Flexible working arrangements can allow workers to devote more time to family and engage in fishing and agriculture for subsistence and sale, continuing what they started during lockdowns. Alternative work hours can also improve livelihood resilience and food security due to the diversified approach tourism workers can take. Survey participants also said they would like more opportunities for training, especially in developing IT, business, or technical skills directed to work outside of the tourism sector in case of future shocks (Scheyvens and Monovo 2020).

(iii) **Resetting the national tourism agenda: adopting a resilience and sustainability approach.** Government support for the tourism sector and its workers has varied across countries. Most workers had to survive without wage subsidies and depleted their retirement savings. This makes them vulnerable and reveals the need for targeted approaches to building resilient financing mechanisms, or a tourism worker insurance or pension scheme.

Some governments are struggling to make loan repayments, including debts on national airline investments and tourism infrastructure. In the meantime, planning offices are planning, pivoting, and resetting the direction of tourism. Some countries take a strategic approach, such as Kiribati, Solomon Islands, and Vanuatu, which are already looking to gain greater value from tourism post-pandemic. Interviews with tourism officials in Fiji, Samoa, Solomon Islands, and Vanuatu revealed a united move toward building domestic market bases and having more control over the direction of tourism to maximize benefits to their people.

In Solomon Islands, the Ministry of Culture and Tourism is thinking innovatively about encouraging domestic tourism by exploring how civil servants' leave entitlements can be adjusted to encourage workers to take a paid holiday in local hotels. Such moves can generate consistent local demand and build a robust domestic tourism base in the region, providing an opportunity for development partners to support the Solomon Islands Tourism Sector Recovery Plan in creating a more circular and resilient tourism base.

Across the Pacific, countries are aligning tourism policies with the SDGs. The Cook Islands, Kiribati, Samoa, Solomon Islands, and Vanuatu are well placed with established guidelines and plans to focus on their people and interests. These countries used the tourism downtime to reflect, consult stakeholders, and engage deliberately in planning for tourism resumption. Conversations with senior tourism officials in Kiribati, Solomon Islands, and Vanuatu, revealed that they now question the "real value of tourism to their people" and are taking steps to "make tourism right for them." Governments in the Pacific are now looking inward, taking a people-first approach that aims to empower and diversify opportunities for local landowning communities to take ownership of tourism and its associated sectors such as agriculture. Countries like Kiribati and the Solomon Islands require immediate financial support to implement sustainable tourism recovery policies and to build a foundation to resume tourism and project sustainable growth into the future. Kiribati is also extending the sustainability agenda through their planned Sustainable Tourism Investment Guidelines, with other countries taking similar measures to integrate tourism and climate considerations.

(iv) **Regional cooperation: pathways toward resilient tourism.** For decades, regionalism has been a central feature in the Pacific, providing strength from which nation-states in the Pacific have negotiated for critical issues globally. In response to the pandemic, SPTO has continued its role as a custodian of the Pacific tourism industry. The Sustainable Tourism Policy Framework and recovery strategy at the SPTO member country and regional levels are key vehicles. However, some limitations with current regional approaches persist, especially regarding support for meaningful action, attainment of the SDGs, and the need to expand the SPTO mandate to reflect its role in climate and pandemic adaptation. SPTO officials interviewed for this project stated a need for ADB to review its bilateral funding arrangements to include regional organizations such as SPTO.

The economic downturn associated with COVID-19 has created significant threats to the Pacific. These threats—which may be beyond the current mandate of SPTO—include financial instability, with many tourism-dependent countries going into high debt, and social instability due to populations struggling to meet their daily needs.

A regional approach to building a resilient Pacific social, economic, and ecological system could provide more effective responses. Pacific Tourism officials say that more accessible regional travel, equitable exchange, and labor mobility between Pacific states could be an avenue to absorb future shocks and create a more connected region.

A long-term and far-reaching approach may be critical to ensuring sustainability and some stability for tourism in the region. The Pacific is under pressure to insulate against known and emerging threats, including climate change-induced displacement, illegal immigration, and poor infrastructures governance. These increasingly complex pressures ultimately require the reexamination of the terms and practicalities of current regional engagement practices, further prompting thinking and planning with a more specific focus on the regional system.

Foremost in taking a systems approach to the problem is the ability to reinvigorate the system by envisioning a shared and SDG-aligned pathway, paving the way for sustainable tourism, fair trade, and resilience. Conversations with key tourism stakeholders show signs that the pandemic is spurring Pacific people to look inward and act on reducing vulnerabilities. ADB is well positioned to recognize the aspirations of destination communities and support plans for sustainable tourism that benefits the region.

Reimagining a Transformation: The Future of Tourism in Thailand

Prepared by Jutamas (Jan) Wisansing, Perfect Link Consulting Group, Thailand

COVID-19 Induced Changes

Before the pandemic, the Thai tourism sector discussed whether its benefits outweighed the unintended consequences associated with its development. Critics questioned whether tourism would improve the quality of life for Thai people in the long term. The concentration of its development within a few stakeholders and destinations became increasingly apparent in the form of high growth first-tier cities. International tourists call those places "their paradise," but local people also experience the negative sides of tourism: increased land prices and costs of living, waste and pollution, and deforestation.

Tourist numbers increased 485% from 1997 to 2019, reaching over 39 million visitors in 2019 (Government of Thailand 2020). This dropped sharply to zero from April to August 2020. This brought some long running challenges to the forefront and helped highlight that Thailand has an opportunity to reimagine a more sustainable industry. This reimagining requires a transformation in the mindset of tourism investors, managers, and policy makers to appreciate that a good place to live will always be a good place to visit and not the other way around. In the following discussion, the government's policy and topics to consider in this transition are described in detail and summed up in Figure 13.

Figure 13: Thematic Areas for Achieving More Sustainable Tourism in Thailand

"a good place to live is a good place to visit"

"a good place to visit is not always a good place to live"

- Sustainable Development Goals
- Rebalancing tourist dispersal
- Reexamining (the neglected) domestic market
  Strengthening Sustainable and Innovative (Domestic) Consumption
- Rebranding Thailand: Sustainable Brand
- Reconnecting to other sectors
  Innovate Tourism PLUS to reach out to other sectors

Source: Authors' compilation.

Opportunities Going Forward

(i)   **Rebalancing tourist dispersal.** COVID-19 impacts were more acute in the main tourist destinations, reflecting (i) their dependence on international visitors, and (ii) that growth in the Thai tourism industry has been highly concentrated geographically, particularly along coasts (such as Pattaya, Phuket, and Samui). The first-tier cities in Thailand also include two urbanized gateways (Bangkok and Chiang Mai). In 2019, 79% of total tourist arrivals visited the southern region, while only 7% (3.5 million) visited the north. In the north, Chiang Mai alone welcomed approximately 3 million foreign visitors (Government of Thailand 2020).

The infrastructure and tourism ecosystem as a whole has been built and driven for international tourism. International travel restrictions have increased competition and price wars but have also led to diversification.

Before the pandemic, the uneven distribution of visitor flows prompted policymakers to embark on a dispersal strategy by shifting marketing from first-tier cities to 55 second-tier cities (Government of Thailand 2019). While international tourists visited first-tier destinations, domestic tourists preferred second-tier destinations, given their accessibility by road. The international market has largely been unaware of—or unattracted to—these destinations, likely due to insufficient infrastructure and accessibility, limited accommodation options, and relatively limited marketing. Marketing for second-tier cities in the past has targeted domestic markets. Pre-COVID-19, the initiative started to see positive dispersal results in the Thai market, creating pathways for improved tourism resilience in the long term.

Pandemic impacts have forced policymakers to redirect efforts to encourage Thai travelers to visit first-tier cities, preventing the collapse of the tourism sector in these destinations. The road to recovery for Thai tourism will therefore be to continue to rebalance tourist dispersal and make an informed decision on marketing investments, particularly to attract the Thai market (domestic tourism) back to first-tier destinations.

(ii)   **Reexamining the domestic market.** Even before the pandemic, domestic tourist numbers outweighed international ones, with 166 million domestic trips in 2019 compared to 40 million international ones. However, domestic travelers stay, on average, 2.5 days, while international tourists stay about 9.5 days. The spending per day of domestic travelers ($71) was less than half of international travelers ($159) in 2018, which explains the focus on international markets.

Given international travel restrictions, however, Thailand repositioned its strategy to invigorate the domestic market. When Thai borders closed in March 2020, resorts and hotels began innovating their marketing strategies based on their understanding of Thai tourist behavior. This focus on the domestic market has helped sustain tourism.

This strategy should continue after the pandemic, to reduce dependency on international markets. For example, the Tourism Authority of Thailand recognized that the expatriate population—specifically Chinese, European, and Japanese—had been largely overlooked. As such, it developed targeted incentives to encourage them to travel and share their domestic tourism experiences with friends, family, and colleagues at home and abroad. Thailand also targeted solo travelers with a special campaign, "Single Travel Route" (Figure 14). Other government's key campaigns such as "We Travel Together" and "Encouragement" (Kum Lung Jai) helped boost the domestic market. Continuing to segment demographics can help achieve the full potential of the domestic Thai market.

Figure 14: Expat Festive Promotion and the Single Journey

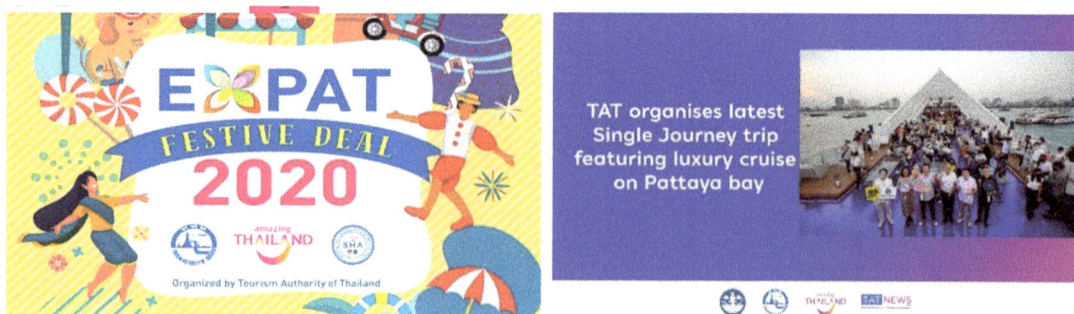

Source: Government of Thailand, Ministry of Tourism and Sports, Tourism Authority of Thailand. 2020. *TAT Highlights Travel Promotions for Expats in Thailand.* Bangkok.

Recovery will depend—in part—on how innovative government authorities and businesses are in stimulating domestic tourism. Given that international tourism may experience prolonged setbacks, this approach can reduce sector vulnerability to the current and future crises.

(iii)   **Rebranding Thailand: increasing value and sustainability in tandem.** Thailand has become one of the most frequently visited destinations in Southeast Asia. The "Land of Smiles" attracts visitors with its excellent food, hospitality, year-round favorable climate, and a diverse landscape of beaches, islands, and mountains. The country has 147 national parks, including 22 national marine parks.

Thailand has developed a reputation as a price-conscious or budget destination. This issue has been debated by the authorities, but stakeholders generally agree that Thailand should move away from its growing dependence on low-yield mass tourism. Chinese tourists, for example, have become the largest market for Thailand, with 10 million visitors in 2018. However, their average per person expenditure in Thailand ($2,026) is lower than their spending in the US ($4,462), and in Japan and the Republic of Korea ($3,000) (Skift 2018). Before the pandemic, the Thai tourism sector sought to address this by rebranding and diversifying services to attract higher spenders in the luxury market.

In addition to focusing on high-end markets, Thailand has started promoting community-based tourism as part of visiting rural destinations. Over 180 communities around Thailand now offer local experiences to introduce visitors to local ways of life. With the diversification in tourism offerings, efforts continue to seek effective ways to build a sustainable tourism brand for Thailand, and identify what exactly constitutes a sustainable brand. Diversifying tourism also bears the risks of introducing tourism to places that are vulnerable and unprepared.

One aspect of vulnerability lies in the geographic features of Thailand and its extensive coastline, as well as exposure to climatic events (Becken and Pant 2019). Further, Thailand has received low rankings on environmental sustainability aspects in the tourism competitiveness index in the past.[5] While recovery currently focuses on the economic dimensions, the discussion should also address how resources are used, preserved, and protected by tourism stakeholders; and how tourism development can actively contribute to the SDGs in Thailand.

(iv)   **Connect tourism to fundamental economic backbones: agriculture and food.** Thailand is one of the major rice producers in the world and the largest rice exporter. Although its best known variety is Thai jasmine rice there are close to 3,500 varieties grown in Thailand, as varied as local wild rice and newly created varieties. However, finding alternative varieties of Thai rice in hotels is rare. There are further opportunities to enhance tourist experiences and understanding of Thai culture through agriculture and the story of food. Stories and marketing can help tourists appreciate the food culture of Thailand in greater depth. Thailand has a range of food-related initiatives, including the "Kitchen to the World", "Amazing Thai Taste" campaigns, and the Michelin Guide Thailand. Further efforts can develop a sustainable culinary supply chain and linkages to other sectors.

Food tourism can extend from production—like agritourism and visits to artisanal food producers—to postconsumption—like value-added souvenir products and food waste management (Wisansing and Berno 2019). Along this continuum are numerous opportunities to engage tourists in a variety of food-related activities and experiences that create socioeconomic benefits for a broad range of stakeholders, many of whom exist outside the primary tourism industry.

(v)   **Sector recovery—how well-prepared is Thailand?** Transforming tourism requires institutional coordination and seamless operations across multiple agencies within the system. Good governance at all levels of government and cooperation with the private sector is key to improve decision-making and create incentives to invest in transformation. An integrated governance structure presents significant challenges

---

[5]   In 2019, Thailand was ranked 130th out of 140 countries with respect to the environmental sustainability of its tourism sector. WEF. 2019. *The Travel and Tourism Competitiveness Report 2019*. Geneva.

to understanding the interlinkages and synergies. Shifting the ideological mindset is critical, and this can be supported by research and development, political champions for change, an integrated authority, and stronger local government involvement.

Thailand is developing its 13th National Economic and Social Development Plan (NESDP) 2023–2027, and the government has accepted two key models for guiding the 13th NESDP: The "Bio-Circular Green Economy" (BCG) model and the "Happy Model". Tourism development can support the 13th NESDP by contributing to the BCG, and conversely, they can support sustainable tourism. Table 6 provides examples of how tourism can support the BCG model.

Table 6: Strategies in the Bio-Circular Green Economy Plan and the Contribution Tourism Can Make

The 2021–2026 BCG Strategic Plan	Rethinking Tourism
Strategy 1: Promoting sustainability of biological resources through balancing conservation and utilization	Rebranding Thailand as a sustainable brand
Strategy 2: Strengthening communities and grassroots economy by employing resource capital, creativity, technology, biodiversity, and cultural diversity to create value to products and services, enabling the communities to move up the value chain	Rebalancing dispersal to distribute benefits. Reexamining domestic markets and consumption and driving innovation.
Strategy 3: Upgrading and promoting sustainable competitiveness of Thai BCG industries with knowledge, technology, and innovation focusing on green manufacturing	Reconnecting to other sectors, enhancing smart farming systems, sustainable culinary tourism, wellness tourism, and responsible tourism. Rebranding Thailand as a sustainable gastronomy destination.
Strategy 4: Building resilience to global changes	Reexamining domestic markets and consumption to achieve innovation and lower dependency on the international market

BCG = bio-circular green economy.
Source: Adapted from Office of National Higher Education Science Research and Innovation Policy Council. 2021. *BCG in Action.*

5   Future Pathways and Opportunities

I n its 2020 Tourism Policy Brief, the United Nations writes that *"…rebuilding tourism is also an opportunity for transformation with a focus on leveraging its impact on destinations visited and building more resilient communities and businesses through innovation, digitalization, sustainability, and partnerships."* The notion of building back better has been promoted widely in the industry, recognizing that *"The pandemic has exposed long standing structural weaknesses in the tourism economy (e.g., fragmented sector, mainly SMEs, seasonality, overdependence, productivity), as well as gaps in government and industry preparedness and response capacity"* (OECD 2021).

A scenario approach is useful for understanding contrasting possible narratives of the future and their implications for sustainable development. This chapter explores different futures, building on the work of the Forum for the Future (2020) and Travalyst (2021). The Forum for the Future (2020) describes four scenarios stemming from COVID-19:

(i)   Discipline—The Age of Technology
(ii)   Compete and Retreat—The End of Globalization?
(iii)   Unsettled—Crisis as the New Normal
(iv)   Transform—A Shift in Mindset

While the Transform scenario delivers the greatest SDG outcomes, readers must understand risks and opportunities under the other scenarios. The remainder of this chapter explores what each future could mean for the ability of tourism to contribute to the SDGs, as well as policy considerations relevant under each scenario (Travalyst 2021).

Discipline—The Age of Technology

The Discipline scenario centers on increased control using digital technology, stricter protocols, and enforcements on *Visitors* and *Industry*. The short-term focus is on maintaining public health and safety, but greater use of technology and standards is also anticipated, which will bring huge volumes of data on every aspect of life and the economy, raising questions of privacy and surveillance. This trajectory also foresees greater automation and a focus on "production efficiency." Remote work will become mainstream in this world, with implications on workplace arrangements, business travel, and well-being (Becken and Hughey 2021). The underpinning mindset of technology and control will not only affect businesses and consumers, but also the *Communities and Culture* element of the tourism system and its relationship with the *Environment*. The goal in this future is to maintain economic growth and globalization, including resuming international travel or recovery "back to normal."

Risks

(i)   Sacrifice consumer privacy and increasing power of governments and a small number of companies over citizens.

(ii)   Missed opportunity to address systemic failures of tourism and economic systems.

(iii)   Exclusion of or disadvantage to some countries, businesses, or travelers.

(iv)   Major investment in digital infrastructure is required, possibly at the expense of other investments.

(v)   Increasing control and standardization puts the existence of diverse cultures at risk.

Opportunities

(i)   Smarter systems can drive operational efficiency at the business level, and this could increase eco-efficiency, for example by reducing wastage.

(ii)   Digital systems can optimize resource use at a network (community) level, for example through smart grids and digitally supported supply chain management.

(iii)   Greater coordination between countries around commonly agreed on standards.

(iv)   Virtual tourism may become more popular, reducing carbon footprints from travel.

(v)   Higher regulation enables governments to raise sustainability and other standards.

(vi)   Voluntary data from consumers can streamline better tourism experiences and aid the formation of "smart destinations."

Emerging Evidence and Policy Implications

Several of the policy responses to the pandemic laid the foundation for a Discipline trajectory, including digital health passports, tracking vaccination or COVID-19 test results, and COVID-19 tracing apps for mobile phones. While some of these measures aim to provide greater transparency and freedom of movement for individuals, they may exacerbate inequalities like unequal access to health treatment. Fostering partnerships among large travel companies in developing countries could encourage cofinancing digital infrastructure.

Investments in touch-free and "seamless" travel technology that started before COVID-19 align with the high-technology narrative. Since the crisis began, 67% of MSMEs have some form of e-commerce to ensure ongoing business activity (Travalyst 2021). Touchless technology—such as voice control and electronic check-ins—will become more prominent in this trajectory. Implications for the workforce (including job losses) and visitors (like feelings of loneliness and lack of connection to destination) need to be managed carefully. Policy needs to be developed to maintain sustainable levels of human-to-human contact in tourism and the required soft skills to provide this (Chapter 2.5).

The need for agreed standards and protocols forms part of the Discipline future. Several organizations have proposed increased regional and global coordination around hygiene and health standards as part of COVID-19 recovery (UNWTO 2020, Twining Ward and McComb 2020). At the same time, tourism-specific hygiene standards have been developed for businesses and destinations, which are already being tested and implemented. These include, for example, the SafeTravels health and hygiene global protocols of the World Travel and Tourism Council, and brand-specific initiatives such as the Hilton CleanStay, or the Accor Cleanliness and Prevention ALLSAFE label.

Countries with higher health standards or existing health and wellness tourism infrastructure might have a competitive advantage (IMF Samoa 2020). Tourism businesses already follow many different types of certification standards—including for sustainability—but at present many of these are voluntary (Griffith University 2014). Those organizations experience a competitive advantage over others that lack experience and capacity to implement standards. This also applies to tourism bodies and government agencies that may not have the experience supporting the sector to implement standardized frameworks. Greater government control of practices could foster sustainability, but also be used to suppress individual choice.

Box 18: Case Study on Hotel Resilient

Hotel Resilient provides a risk-based standard for hotels and resorts, that are supported by online software with options for training and consulting. To address the coronavirus disease (COVID-19) pandemic, Hotel Resilient has developed a COVID-19-ready standard and certification, as well as a multihazard and climate change standard and certification. The latter applies to all types of risks, allowing hotels and resorts to implement a risk management framework relevant to their unique business risk, covering over 250 indicators that guide hotels to assess and implement risk and resilience measures. Certification thus provides reassurance to guests that the hotel is safe and able to manage crisis situations.

Source: Hotel Resilient.

Improved standardization and certification will increase transparency for visitors while also providing an opportunity to better integrate sustainability aspects, such as the responsible use of water when implementing hygiene and sanitation measures.

Increasing and sharing tourism data and statistics can strengthen the ability of tourism to deliver on the SDGs; as long as data cover metrics that inform progress on SDGs (Chapter 2.5). Governments play a key role in providing data infrastructure and communication to the sector, and this needs to be scaled up to account for the "true cost" of tourism.

The Discipline future will require substantial investment in digital innovation, infrastructure, and capability—from internet connectivity to business training—and greater emphasis on computing science in education (UN 2020). Small businesses with limited financial or human capacity may be disadvantaged and MSMEs will require support in establishing a digital presence. There will also be an urgent need to upskill workers on cybersecurity.

Compete and Retreat—The End of Globalization?

The Compete and Retreat trajectory sees a future of strengthened nationalism—or potentially regionalism—and a decline of global approaches and solidarity. This trajectory follows a mindset that resources are scarce and national interests dominate, with borders controlled tightly. Domestic travel will be the main form of tourism. Feelings of unity, national identity, and patriotism might grow as community cohesiveness increases. Countries will prioritize their economies and investment in self-sufficiency. Countries with fewer natural resources may face difficulties as the global economy contracts, and the use of unsustainable materials like coal may increase. On the other hand, reduced international travel and trade could limit global transportation networks and emissions. All VICE elements would change substantially, especially the *Visitor* and *Community* dimensions.

Risks

(i)   Growing inequality between countries as some will be heavily impacted by reduced international travel, and because some are more self-sufficient.

(ii)   Higher inefficiency and unsustainability as countries revert to national solutions rather than benefitting from global technology or resources.

(iii) Competing approaches to sustainability and multiple standards that are confusing to international consumers.
(iv) Limited exchange of information, data, and knowledge will hamper progress on finding the most effective sustainability solutions.

Opportunities

(i)   Increased "localism" and community resilience.
(ii)   Revival of cultural practices and identity.
(iii) Local supply chains reduce leakage and are buffered against external disruptions.
(iv) Reduced international aviation and transport will decrease greenhouse gas emissions.

Emerging Evidence and Policy Implications

In the immediate COVID-19 response, many countries found themselves focused on a national approach, for example by closing borders, prioritizing national citizens (over migrant workers or visitors), providing support to national companies and "anchor businesses," and securing vaccines for their people (Twining Ward and McComb 2020). Promoting domestic tourism was not so much a preference as a necessity, and regional travel "bubbles" followed. Long-term patterns might emerge from this shift, leading to a permanent contraction in global mobility. Not every country has the same access to a domestic or regional market and as a result, tourism in some destinations will shrink in this scenario.

There is considerable evidence on the implications of domestic travel in India and Thailand. Before COVID-19, India had already come up with an innovative campaign called *Dekho Apna Desh* (See Your Country) to encourage domestic tourism. Citizens can pledge to visit at least 15 domestic destinations by 2022 to win a prize (Government of India 2020). The Thai government, for example, invested $700 million to incentivize domestic tourism (IMF Samoa 2020).

Investment in government services—including digital infrastructure, attractions, or natural systems—might be the beginning of internally focused political priorities. Investment in green infrastructure is imperative in this scenario. In response to foreign workers returning to their home countries, the International Labour Organization recommends governments consider "effective return and reintegration policies" (ILO 2020). Ongoing communication with the local population, businesses, and workers is important to address heightened social tensions and uncertainty.

Several organizations recommend diversifying national economies and considering shorter supply chains that are not exposed to external volatility. One approach is to focus on capturing tourism benefits for local people by shifting toward local procurement and reducing economic leakage (UN 2020, Australasian British Travel Association 2021). Opportunities lie in greater partnerships between national and local governments, including community engagement (Travalyst 2021). Communities might become more empowered in this scenario, and governments can actively support this through capacity building and by ensuring that funds are available for communities to administer.

National approaches may be extended to regional ones; but in either case transport, hospitality and insurance sectors will need to coordinate closely to respond to the changing health contexts within countries (IMF 2021). Current moves by both the Australian and British governments to subsidize domestic air travel are not only pointing toward policy preferences of supporting national economies, but also a return to "business as usual" with heavy dependence on air travel (Topham 2021). Investments in greener transport networks could encourage a long-term shift from air to land.

**Box 19: Case Study on Regional Cooperation of Small Businesses
in the Greater Mekong Subregion**

The Mekong Tourism Coordinating Office (MTCO) was established with funding from the six Greater Mekong Subregion (GMS) members—Cambodia, the Lao People's Democratic Republic, Myanmar, the People's Republic of China, Thailand, and Viet Nam. The two functions of MTCO are to coordinate sustainable tourism development projects in the Mekong and to promote the Mekong region as a single destination.

The MTCO is active on multiple fronts, but what stood out in response to the coronavirus disease (COVID-19) was its ability to connect small businesses from the countries, and to coordinate information exchange among governments. The "managed collaboration," according to Jens Thraenhart, MTCO chief executive officer, has been successful because it was initiated from the grassroots, and not top-down. The brand of the MTCO is collectively owned by small businesses that "feel they are part of something." This not only strengthens a sense of community but also builds resilience and capability through business-to-business learning.

For governments, the network has become an important source of information and a platform to coordinate initiatives and policies. It has also built an effective mechanism for the public and private sectors to work together more closely, by way of building trust and partnerships.

Several working groups focus on topics such as agritourism, wellness tourism, sustainability and climate action, and research and data. An advisory group provides an opportunity for a wide range of experts and stakeholders to provide input and be directly connected to the strategy development of the organization. The COVID-19 crisis highlighted the benefit of an already existing structure that provided communication channels for effective crisis management.

Source: Mekong Tourism. 2021. *Lao PDR: New Project to Protect Landscapes and Enhance Livelihoods.*

Unsettled—Crisis as the New Normal

This future is not so much defined by a particular mindset, but by the ongoing impact of crisis and uncertainty. The trajectory will move from one shock to another, including those related to resource scarcity, extreme climatic events, and conflict. Travalyst labels this future "The end of tourism as we know it," highlighting that the uncertainty associated with such a volatile world will make travel and business very difficult, thus particularly impacting the *Visitor, Industry,* and *Community* dimensions (Travalyst 2021). Economically and psychologically, people will be less inclined to engage in tourism, as communities are forced to deal with immediate problems instead of tourism. Recovery and reconstruction efforts will be hampered by new failures. These may be related to COVID-19 in the short term, such as insufficient vaccination, mutations, and setbacks in opening borders. Issues may also be compounded by the impacts of other events, such as recessions, competition between countries (like water wars), or extreme weather events. Action to achieve SDGs will become challenging. Thus, it will not be the size, strength, or wealth of businesses determining success in future markets, but their adaptive capacity (Barkas et al. 2020).

Risks

(i)   Mounting economic damage from crises, forcing actors into a responsive pattern, eroding proactive and long-term measures toward sustainability.
(ii)   Multicrisis management will be very costly.

(iii)   Significant restructuring of the global travel system will become necessary.

(iv)   Vulnerable groups will be affected more and require special support.

(v)   Building back consumer confidence—especially for international travelers—will be challenging.

Opportunities

(i)   Destinations with closer markets may benefit as people still want to holiday, just not so far away from home.

(ii)   People might demand authentic experiences that ground them in nature or culture.

(iii)   New products around healing and well-being might be in high demand.

(iv)   Resource scarcity and crisis might result in greater efficiency and optimization of how they are consumed and produced.

Emerging Evidence and Policy Implications

Several organizations recognize the need to increase the resilience of tourism, not only to pandemics but to other crises. The Organisation for Economic Co-operation and Development (OECD) suggests introducing a "periodic review of jurisdictional responsibilities to ensure flexibility in the system, and to further strengthen institutional capacity at destination level" (OECD 2020). Thus, improving governance is a key measure to increase the ability of tourism to respond to disruptions. The World Bank also recommends building institutional capacity to "bolster resilience and facilitate faster rebound" (Twining Ward and McComb 2020). Other authorities recommend establishing a central "nerve center" for tourism to bring together public and private actors around a collaborative framework for decision-making (McKinsey & Company 2020).

Governments will be under increasing pressure to deliver social safety nets versus financial prudence and mounting public debt. Larger infrastructure projects might be difficult to fund, undermining the opportunity for some forms of tourism. Similarities in building requirements allowed tourism businesses to repurpose their facilities during the pandemic, such as to accommodate health workers, homeless people, or people in quarantine. Future policies should consider building standards that mandate multipurpose approaches.

Others suggest measures of diversifying products, destinations, and economic structures, which will be challenging for destinations that have limited resources, for example, island states (ADB 2020). These measures will be important, especially for small island developing states, as they already experience multiple layers of crisis. Fiji, for example, was struck by several severe cyclones at the end of 2020 and the beginning of 2021 while responding to the pandemic. While resilient to a certain point, some tourism destinations or businesses might need support with exit strategies to cut losses (The Commonwealth 2020).

Destination risk assessments should be undertaken to create early warning systems (Government of New Zealand 2021). Overdependence on tourism is a key factor that exposes countries to a future crisis, especially when the country depends on international travel. The extent to which governments have supported air travel represents a risky return to a mode of transport that presents long-term climate risk. Airline support packages that do not incentivize carbon reduction are missing an important opportunity to accelerate the much needed decarbonization of transport systems. New Zealand is setting a positive example by exploring a different approach to decarbonization, by discussing a departure tax to offset the environmental cost of flying (Hunt 2021). Using recovery after COVID-19 to incentivize technological innovation or modal shifts in tourism will be important to futureproofing the sector.

Transforming business models, including remote and flexible work arrangements, are further options for addressing the crisis (ILO 2020, Travalyst 2021). New models are already emerging that increase the adaptability of tourism businesses. In the early stages of the pandemic, tourism workers with transferable skills deployed to other sectors or redesigned their products to address the needs of the local population. Examples include cooking and delivering meals to people in isolation, selling products at food stalls, or providing educational tours to schools. The future tourism workforce will benefit from greater flexibility and agility when people are forced to move jobs or change careers. New policy frameworks are required to enable a more resilient business and work environment (UN 2020).

Protecting the consumer may be increasingly necessary for a highly uncertain future. It is important to consider improvements in cancellation policies or travel insurance (WTTC 2020). Drawing on data from Trip.com, Travalyst reports that 57% of customers put forward penalty-free cancellation policies as important elements when booking their travel (Travalyst 2020). To provide effective responses to a reoccurring crisis, international cooperation will also be important (Chapter 2.5). For example, discussing the recovery of the Maldives, ADB suggested that "enhanced participation in the international community is necessary to achieve coordination in travel protocols and ensure that the travel and tourism sectors in the Maldives survive in the 'new normal'." (ADB 2020).

Box 20: Case Study on Resilient Community-Based Tourism in Baan Talae Nok, Thailand

Baan Talae Nok on the Andaman Coast in southern Thailand has developed a resilient community-based tourism model. The community relies on the local mangrove forest, which Mossberg (2021) says, "is like a supermarket for the villagers, […] it provides crustaceans, mollusks, crabs and fish." The villagers don't see conservation as something restrictive, rather it means they use the natural resources in a sustainable way so that they will continue to benefit their children. The local population also understands that the forests—if healthy—act as an ecotourism attraction. Villagers are welcoming tourists to their homes, their way of life, handicrafts, and the unspoiled nature of the area. Tourists appreciate the opportunity to connect with the local people and gain an authentic experience.

The pandemic affected tour operators in the region with cancellations from international tourists; however, the Baan Talae Nok community shows strong signs of resilience. Thanks to their ability to live off natural resources, villagers can feed their families and still generate income from selling some of the seafood. The remoteness and vast environment surrounding the destination also means that infections have remained low, as there is limited traffic of people. The uncertainty of not knowing when tourists will return does affect the local people, as does the fact that they are missing the cultural exchange with tourists. However, the fact that the destination is remote and naturally provides safety and social distancing suggests that it will be sought after once travel resumes.

Sources: E. Mossberg. 2021. Host Communities Are at the Core of Tomorrow's Sustainable Tourism. *The Good Tourism Blog.* 28 January; and Authors.

Transform—A Shift in Mindset

The Transform future requires the largest shift in mindset and economic systems across all VICE elements of the tourism system. The focus of this trajectory is progress toward a more sustainable, low-carbon, fair, and equitable world. It requires transitioning away from exploitative practices to regenerative ones—changes required to achieve this are not incremental, but transformational.

Collective action—both locally and globally—is required across all types of actors. Key elements include a shift in perspective from anthropocentrism to environmental ethics, a move from a growth paradigm to one of stewardship, and abandoning the notion of price to make way for value (Dwyer 2018). As described by the Forum for the Future

"For a company that serves society, profit is the means, not the goal in itself. Wellbeing is a measure of success, and so is resilience. Inequality is not a by-product of the system but a metric of failure."

Risks

(i)   Not all countries are in a similar position to transition away from high-carbon or extractive industries.
(ii)   The transition needs to be managed well to ensure that vulnerable groups are not disadvantaged or left behind.
(iii)   Those who are not able to adapt to new models or values may go out of business.
(iv)   There might be opposition to change.

Opportunities

(i)   A greater focus on thriving and well-being could address other issues, such as those related to physical and mental health.
(ii)   Rapid action on climate change will help reduce the risk of climate disasters and prevent loss of life and capital.
(iii)   Increased community cohesion will lead to healthy and resilient destinations.
(iv)   People reconnect to nature and enjoy a revival of natural ecosystems, including clean rivers and air, and abundant wildlife.
(v)   An increase in demand for nature tourism and sustainable experiences will further enhance business practices and products.

Emerging Evidence and Policy Implications

Transforming tourism requires considerable effort at all scales: local, national, regional, and global. Enhancing diversity and inclusiveness in tourism is a key step toward delivering on the SDGs. To achieve this, governments must ensure adequate representation of minority groups in decision-making processes (WTTC 2020). Measurement and reporting of progress in sustainable transitions from or through tourism are also critical (ABTA 2021).

At the local level, the importance of "destination stewardship [...] to drive action for preservation of cultural and natural assets" has been recognized by the World Travel and Tourism Council in their recommendations to support local voices and foster local public–private–community partnerships (Chapter 2.3) (WTTC 2021). The Mana Tiaki Certification Program in the Cook Islands is an excellent example of a community values-driven initiative that seeks to improve the sustainability of tourism and connect visitors and locals alike to the uniqueness of the place. While its initial driver was tourism-focused, it has now helped bring the community together on other sustainability initiatives. Another example is Kiwi Welcome—initiated in Queenstown, New Zealand—where tourists buy a membership that gives them access to discounts from local tourism businesses. All profits go to preserving the land and community, and tourists are connected to businesses that care about their unique place.

Box 21: Case Study on the Global Himalayan Expedition–Trekking Tourism with an Impact

In 2013, an entrepreneurial Indian engineer started a sustainable development firm called Global Himalayan Expedition (GHE). The core idea was to attract customers for "impact expeditions," in which trekkers carry solar panels to remote regions and use their fees to raise funds for community projects. Since then, the concept helped install solar power in 131 villages of three regions in India, changing the lives of more than 60,000 people. In 2020, GHE became one of 13 companies to win a UN Global Climate Action award, as "one of the world's first organizations using the force of tourism coupled with technology to bring solar energy to remote communities."

continued

Box 21: *continued*

The business model of a "built-in" benefit through tourism aligns with the Transform future. The pandemic reduced the number of trekking customers, so the company diversified into working with destinations on a range of initiatives. Importantly, GHE established a partnership with offsetting company South Pole to provide cleaner cooking stoves to families in remote villages; typically, those that GHE already worked with on electrification. Attracting interest from large corporates, GHE is now connecting providers and consumers of carbon credits with development in rural areas, providing visitors (and others purchasing carbon credits) with better experiences, including a carbon certificate, and enhancing the sustainability of the community destination. The latter is achieved through additional initiatives such as supplying local health centers with solar energy—which is increasingly demanded by travelers after the pandemic—and increases the standard of living of the locals.

Sources: Authors; Forum for the Future. 2020. *From System Shock to System Change: Time to Transform the Future of Sustainability.* England.

Finance and funding for more environmentally friendly tourism infrastructure will be critical in this scenario. The International Finance Corporation has created an online certification platform to assist the construction of green enterprises called Excellence in Design for Greater Efficiencies (Destination Thailand News 2021). Destination Capital—a hotel investment group headquartered in Bangkok—has launched a "green hotel fund", using the International Finance Corporation platform. It is the first fund in the world to encourage sustainability investments for tourism. Further opportunities around green bonds for tourism, including for aviation, need to be explored as critical enablers of the transition away from carbon. The OECD recommends investing in sustainable aviation fuels but also suggests a transfer from air to rail where possible (OECD 2020). Exit strategies for high emitters may be necessary.

The World Bank-funded Lao PDR Landscapes and Livelihoods Project supports the Lao PDR's COVID-19 recovery by securing livelihoods and jobs from managing forests sustainably, including through opportunities created from nature-based tourism, while protecting natural capital and securing important ecosystem services (Mekong Tourism 2021). As a transition mechanism toward decarbonization, there is an opportunity to generate funds from tourism and direct them toward carbon sequestration and forest restoration. As such, carbon offsetting can contribute to SDG 13 and SDG 15, and even SDG 14 in the case of blue carbon.[6] Tourism will benefit from wider sustainability investments such as the Clean and Sustainable Ocean Partnership led by ADB and the European Investment Bank to support initiatives in Asia and the Pacific to advance the SDGs and the climate goals of the Paris Agreement (ADB 2021). The partnership will focus on reducing marine plastic pollution; promoting clean waterways, sustainable management, protection, and restoration of marine and coastal ecosystems; and supporting disaster risk preparedness, green shipping, ports, and maritime infrastructure.

To enable economic reform, governments need to incentivize sustainable practices, consider the potential climate impact of fiscal recovery policies, attach sustainability criteria to public investments, advance evidence and science-based policy, and invest in the measurement of sustainable tourism (Chapter 2.5) (WTTC 2020, Hepburn et al. 2020, UN 2020). Circular economy principles need to be mainstreamed to reduce waste, pollution, and external costs (OECD 2020). The UN recommends establishing "work-for-nature" schemes, including those that catalyze entrepreneurship and female employment (UNWTO 2021). All of these can be supported through deeper coordination and collaboration (Chapter 2.5).

---

[6]   Blue carbon projects focus on carbon sequestration in marine environments, including through planting mangroves and leveraging tidal marshes and seagrass to achieve decarbonization.

Box 22: Case Study on Regenerative Tourism

New Zealand set up a Tourism Futures Taskforce to use the "pause in tourism" for the long-term benefit of the country. The 6-month consultation process resulted in a new vision for tourism. The taskforce recognized a need to abandon an "industry that is focused on the dollar" and Maori culture that "has been undervalued and undersold", and to move toward a future visitor economy that is regenerative and resilient. Benefits need to arise across all four components of well-being: social, cultural, environmental, and economic. Practically, the future of Aotearoa tourism must enrich visitors, contribute to the health of local communities, provide meaningful work, draw on Te Ao Māori (Maori worldviews), improve the health of natural ecosystems, and produce durable financial returns. New Zealand is also supporting indigenous-to-indigenous networks by investing in linking Maori entrepreneurs with startups in other Pacific island countries, as they share common philosophies and alternative business models, which can support cothriving and development.

Source: Government of New Zealand, Ministry of Business, Innovation, and Employment. 2020. *Tourism Futures Taskforce.*

Box 23: Case Study on Planet Happiness

Planet Happiness is an initiative by the Happiness Alliance. It intends to use tourism as a vehicle for destination sustainability and positively contribute to the well-being of host communities. The founders support the view that holistic measures of success for tourism are needed, rather than a narrow focus on economic metrics. Planet Happiness has developed a methodology and supporting resources for tourism decision-makers and destination stakeholders to guide tourism planning and development centered on creating well-being for host communities. The Happiness Index, which has been recognized by the OECD, is a critical element of this methodology.

The Happiness Index is based on Bhutan's model of Gross National Happiness and consists of 11 well-being domains: community; environment; life-long learning, arts, and culture; psychological well-being; government; health; standard of living, economy; social support; time balance; satisfaction with life; and work. Questions have also been added on tourism and its contribution to local development. Indicators measure subjective happiness in each domain, and these are mapped against the SDGs. It is noted that measuring progress toward the SDGs alone may not provide an accurate indication of happiness. The Happiness Index thus complements the SDGs. Results inform what policies and initiatives can strengthen linkages between tourism development and enhancing the quality of life of residents.

Aside from tourism planning, the Happiness Index can support government decision-making on a broader scale. Because the index measures individual happiness, each participant receives a personal scorecard, which compares their scores against destination-wide results. Residents found the happiness (and SDG) agenda more relevant because the index puts well-being at the center and raises awareness about personal happiness, community well-being, and tourism. The connection between personal and destination well-being scores facilitates discussions and increases community participation in developing and implementing interventions.

Planet Happiness works specifically with World Heritage Sites and their partners to manage overtourism while supporting the cultural and environmental agendas. Examples include the following:

(i)   Australia: Central Victorian Goldfields, with the Goldfields World Heritage bid project
(ii)   Indonesia: Cultural Landscapes of Bali, Borobudur, and Komodo National Park, with the Bali Tourism Polytechnic
(iii)   Nepal: Mt. Everest National Park, with the Himalayan Trust
(iv)   Thailand: Sukhothai and Ayutthaya, with the Thai National Government Designated Areas for Sustainable Tourism Administration
(v)   Viet Nam: Hoi An, with Danang Architect University

Another example of the work of Planet Happiness is with the Vanuatu Department of Tourism on how to redesign tourism as part of the COVID-19 recovery. These discussions inform investments and policy design for a purposeful restart.

Source: The Happiness Alliance.

6 Recommendations for Decision-Makers

Overview

Tourism has grown so fast that it has overwhelmed many of the systems set up to manage it. Although there is considerable government involvement in tourism, interventions have focused on supporting revenue growth and building prestige, rather than encouraging sustainable development. Communities and the environment have paid the price for under-regulation and limited governance. COVID-19 has brought to the foreground the "underbelly" of tourism in Asia and the Pacific, such as overdependence, limited control over sector growth, external costs, and labor market challenges including skills gaps and limited rights of workers. The pandemic affords unique opportunities to evaluate sector progress and address its most pressing issues.

The term "build back better" is often used when describing the recovery of tourism. The region, however, should not seek to recapture the tourism of the prepandemic era but rather "build *forward* better." This means creating a new kind of tourism that is more closely aligned with the Sustainable Development Goals.

Transforming tourism so that it genuinely contributes to achieving the SDGs will require a mix of incentives and disincentives. Disincentives will include legislation to restrict unsustainable practices and fast-track alternatives. Some examples are emission standards, employee protection schemes, green building standards, and policy tools to internalize environmental costs or phase out harmful materials and technologies. Legislation should help create equal treatment and support elements of tourism that drive sustainability, for example, community engagement. Incentives may include policies and investments to support innovation and the development of green infrastructure, encourage behavior change, and leverage digital technology and big data more effectively.

Among the most pressing barriers to sustainable tourism in the region is the lack of good governance structures to support long-term planning, collaboration, and management. Establishing more inclusive and sustainability-oriented governance frameworks and using them to strengthen coordination and stakeholder management will be necessary for tourism development in line with the SDGs. There is also a pressing need to include the voices of marginalized groups in tourism development, including those of communities, the informal economy, and small businesses. Establishing clear accountability frameworks and other mechanisms to demonstrate progress is essential.

Ultimately, implementation will depend largely on financing. Given the cross sectoral nature of tourism, it is important to explore opportunities for cofinancing projects and sharing resources across sectors, such as through nature-based solutions, sustainable livelihoods, and green infrastructure projects. For instance, tourism will never fully deliver on the sustainability agenda if low-carbon aviation fuels are not mainstreamed, and accommodation venues will struggle to achieve environmental sustainability in the absence of clean power. Although fuel and renewable energy are beyond the immediate scope of tourism, there are considerable opportunities for collaboration. Tourism stakeholders can lobby for sustainable products and services, while counterparts can help finance infrastructure and provide services that enable tourism to deliver on the Sustainable Development Goals.

Shifting tourism to a more sustainable development pathway will not happen by chance, and political interests will seek to prevent change. Accordingly, this report advances six pathways to foster systemic change:

(i)   value-driven tourism,
(ii)   decarbonizing tourism,
(iii)   tourism-led regeneration,
(iv)   diversification,
(v)   improving tourism governance, and
(vi)   aligning tourism finance with sustainability.

Each pathway offers recommendations on how policymakers can guide tourism to contribute more effectively to the SDGs. Many of the recommendations will also be relevant to the private sector and development partners. Since country contexts and tourism sectors differ substantially, not all recommendations are equally relevant for all. Governments may focus on the pathways and recommendations that align best with their tourism and development strategies. Overall, establishing a more sustainable trajectory will require intervention across all elements of tourism, including the visitor, industry, community, and environment dimensions (captured in the VICE model), as well as collaboration across the public and private sectors, development partners, communities, and destinations.

Value-Driven Tourism

(i)   **Focus on quality and yield.** Destinations can benefit from attracting visitors that spend more, or who want to interact genuinely with destinations, communities, and the environment. One way of attracting this type of visitor is to **develop tourism products that add value** and leverage local resources responsibly. Nature walks, hosted by local guides, are one example; these have high service components and can offer rich and authentic experiences. Governments can encourage innovation and the development of new products by supporting incubators, providing start-up funding, and establishing business awards. It will be necessary to **provide training that focuses on high-quality services** to prepare the workforce to engage with high-value markets. Crucially, there is a need to **address supply chain issues and reduce economic leakage** to ensure local businesses and MSMEs receive a greater share of business benefits. Further, where tourism creates external costs for communities or the environment, policymakers may consider applying the "polluter pays" principle or similar mechanisms to internalize costs, so that the "net value" remains positive.

(ii)   **Manage carrying capacity.** As new destinations emerge and existing ones develop, it is essential to **understand their socioecological limits** and to manage tourism accordingly. Adequate data, planning, and enforcement are all critical for ensuring that destination resources are managed responsibly. Destination marketing should shift both community and visitor perspectives from viewing places as resources to be exploited toward **natural and social assets that should be cultivated**. Digital technology can help monitor tourist flows and support resource management.

(iii)   **Leverage uniqueness of place.** Tourism products should be informed by—and respect—unique local culture and natural resources. Policies should **encourage appropriate at-place design** of buildings, infrastructure, and experiences. Some examples include the use of natural airflow and shade to cool buildings or the selection of local vegetation for gardens. To leverage the unique features of destinations, stakeholders can **develop place-sensitive destination management strategies** that consider local assets and look for ways to address context-specific challenges, including the protection of culture.

(iv)   **Measure success.** Governments and other stakeholders should use sustainability indicators that **measure the holistic contribution of tourism to development efforts**. It is also important to report on progress in a transparent manner, leveraging data sharing where possible to improve monitoring and evaluation and to share lessons.

Decarbonizing Tourism

(i) **Design and implement decarbonization policies for tourism. Carbon reduction pathways with clear targets** are an essential foundation for designing climate policies and monitoring their success. Policy levers can help scale up renewable energy generation or the use of biomaterials to decarbonize the tourism industry (Chapter 4.3). Development partners and governments can support decarbonization by investing in innovation, supporting long-term commitments and partnerships, and helping pilot new approaches. Governments should also **consider economic and fiscal instruments**, like carbon taxes or hypothecating resources for climate mitigation, **to decouple growth from emissions**. In addition to economic tools, countries may consider including tourism, aviation, and shipping targets in their nationally determined contributions or development plans. Doing so can help account for and manage the carbon footprint of travel to a country and may support accessing international climate finance (Chapter 2.5).

(ii) **Take a collaborative approach to sustainable aviation fuels.** Transport emissions remain a key issue for decarbonizing tourism, and mainstream adoption of sustainable aviation fuels will require funding for ongoing research and development, and upscaling. **Development partners can help build consortia to distribute or underwrite associated risks** while supporting knowledge sharing. As sustainable fuels become more prevalent, governments should consider developing fuel standards, such as fuel-blend mandates, and collaborate to increase the adoption of fuel standards.

(iii) **Raise awareness and build carbon literacy.** Education and training can help build carbon literacy among businesses and government officials. **Carbon labeling** schemes and reporting mechanisms will also be critical for making visitors more aware of their carbon footprint. Developing programs for guests, including **visitor pledges** and low-carbon transport options and visitor experiences, can support the adoption of low carbon behavior.

(iv) **Enable lower carbon industry practices.** Governments can implement **certification schemes or industry standards linked to business licensing,** or provide incentives tied to decarbonization (Chapter 2.2). Awards for low carbon businesses can help reinforce best practices and encourage innovation. Setting minimum regulatory requirements, such as emission standards for vehicles or energy efficiency standards, can decrease the use of high-emitting technologies and practices.

Tourism-Led Regeneration

(i) **Foster ecological restoration. Tourism can support improved resource management and environmental stewardship.** To achieve this, governments can encourage visitor and industry contributions through donations and volunteering opportunities, or by establishing specific **regeneration taxes** (Chapter 2.5). Another option is to integrate sustainability and restoration activities into licenses or concessions for tourism in national parks (Chapter 2.2). Subsidies and educational activities can encourage businesses to **improve the supply and efficiency of water and energy resources;** or to prioritize nature-based solutions—including for climate change adaptation—where feasible (Chapter 2.4) The public and private sectors can collaborate to build businesses around the circular economy and connect these to the visitor economy, which can further support the growth of sustainable products and markets (Chapter 5.4).

(ii) **Protect communities and encourage cultural thriving.** Tourism can help preserve cultural traditions and practices but needs to be managed such that communities are protected and respected, and not exploited. To achieve this, **communities need to have a voice in the development** of tourism activity. Governments should implement good practice standards for cultural events and—more broadly—**develop ethical standards for how the tourism industry uses culture**, particularly for marketing and product development. Ethical standards should consider "whose story it is to tell" and ensure that intellectual property rights are protected. There are also considerable opportunities to leverage tourism to encourage entrepreneurship and business activity among indigenous people. **Mentorship programs and business grants can support local entrepreneurs** to get established and grow. Development partners and governments should also seek to **support indigenous-to-indigenous (or "I2I") networks** where possible (Box 7 and Box 22).

(iii) **Ensure tourism is inclusive and supports health and subjective well-being.** Decision-making processes that affect sector development should include all voices, including those of women and indigenous groups, and monitoring frameworks should include gender- and diversity-specific indicators. For visitor inclusion, governments may wish to address discriminating visa restrictions to ensure equitable access to travel (Chapter 2.1). Stakeholders can also **invest in social tourism** to enable underprivileged groups to participate in travel. Similarly, **investing in accessible and inclusive experiences in nature** can further expand access. Tourism can contribute to subjective well-being by **building connectedness with nature through education programs,** family holiday activities, or guided tours with indigenous guides (Chapter 5.4). For health, **proactive risk management and health and safety standards** are essential to ensuring visitor and employee safety (Box 18). Industry good practice standards should consider the well-being of workers and can be implemented in partnership with global or regional organizations (Chapter 4.1).

(iv) **Empower local communities and MSMEs.** To address economic inclusion, tourism should **encourage genuine participation from businesses of all sizes**, including those run by vulnerable or minority groups. Governments can **incentivize innovation and product development with competitions, incubators,** and supportive policies. Public and private sector actors should build networks and local partnerships that include smaller businesses (Box 19). Development organizations can also foster community entrepreneurship and innovation through capacity building, training, and funding support. Specific **training areas may focus on digital technology but also soft skills** to manage tourism (Chapter 2.5). Development partners can also add value by strengthening local government capacity to identify and act on opportunities in sustainable tourism.

Diversification

(i) **Diversify markets.** Overdependence on a specific market segment—such as international visitors—creates exposure to external shocks. **Revising destination marketing strategies can help reduce dependence on dominant markets** (Chapter 5.2). Policymakers may wish to build or strengthen closer to home markets and align markets with the DNA of local destinations, to ensure socioecological carrying capacities are respected.

(ii) **Diversify products.** Tourism markets should increasingly **develop products for domestic visitors** (Chapter 4.3). Policymakers may also wish to encourage experiences that "give back," such as community projects or ones that fulfill community needs (Box 21). **Localizing supply chains**—for example by encouraging hotels (at the point of licensing) to procure from local businesses or communities—can support product diversification and inclusion of local MSMEs (Chapter 5.2). Tourism stakeholders should also **explore opportunities for flexible assets** such as popup structures or multipurpose buildings.

(iii) **Support workforce diversity and expand skills.** Employers can foster diversity at the workplace by actively encouraging minority groups to apply and developing company policies that support vulnerable employees. Job training and education should provide soft skills and **prepare for "workplace flexibility"** (Chapter 2.5). Employers can also help **develop transferrable skills** that enable workers to explore career paths both in and outside of the industry. One example is training staff as "first response" personnel to support emergency management systems.

(iv) **Foster economic diversification.** Economies with heavy dependence on tourism should protect themselves from future shocks by seeking opportunities for economic diversification. Policymakers should seek to remove biases that favor tourism over other industries and look for ways to integrate tourism into parallel sectors, like agriculture and health (Chapter 4.3). The public sector can support businesses not capable of surviving shocks to develop exit strategies.

Improving Tourism Governance

(i)   **Integrate policy considerations across sectors.** Given the crosscutting nature of tourism, it is important to **build a deeper understanding of tourism in nontourism government departments** through education and awareness raising. This will help to integrate tourism considerations in nontourism policies (e.g., climate change) (Chapter 2.5). Cross-government collaboration and alignment are also needed to address some of the pressing tourism challenges, including supporting or formalizing the "informal" tourism economy (Chapter 2.2). Governments can help develop enabling ecosystems that foster industry innovation and sustainability.

(ii) **Foster cooperation and public-private collaboration.** Collaboration needs to take place more actively across countries, sectors, governments, and businesses. Governments and development partners can **support deeper coordination on data harmonization, monitoring and evaluation, and investments** through framework agreements and projects. Cofinancing and public–private partnerships are key tools for scaling up such networked collaboration and cooperation. Public actors can also foster information sharing by supporting local stakeholder networks and by **encouraging industry actors to participate in sector planning.** Policies developing global and regional guidelines—such as **sustainability standards—** can increase coordinated action between countries while also informing national and local guidelines. Furthermore, countries can take cooperative approaches to reduce competitive pressures, more efficiently allocate scarce resources, and increase marketing on the uniqueness of place (Chapter 4.2) Connecting sustainability concepts with local worldviews or religions can help to cultivate a shared understanding and common language between community stakeholders, governments, and the private sector.

(iii) **Invest in strategy, marketing, and technology.** One of the key investments governments can make is in **building human capacity to effectively plan and implement more sustainable tourism**. There are further **investment needs in the areas of ethical marketing** that follow a sustainability strategy. Investments in digital technology can support monitoring and implementation but should include safeguards to ensure ethical use of data and the avoidance of unintended consequences such as job loss (Box 12).

(iv) **Build capacity in disaster risk management and adaptation.** As the tourism industry continues to change, one of the most important skills for both the public and private sectors will be the ability to adapt and respond to crises. Early warning systems and effective communication systems are key to saving lives and assets on which tourism depends. Educators and employers should build capacity in **future thinking and adaptive pathway management** and encourage ongoing learning in response to new disasters. Governments and development partners should seek to create strategic links between the tourism and humanitarian sectors to help **redeploy resources as new crises emerge** (Chapter 5.3).

Aligning Tourism Finance with Sustainability

(i)   **Seek new revenue sources which support sustainable tourism.** With the fiscal impact of COVID-19, it will be important for national governments to seek new sources of financing that also serve their goals on sustainable tourism. Fiscal instruments like carbon taxes can reduce the carbon footprint of transport for tourism. These form part of a wider portfolio of pricing mechanisms for tourism that provide sustainable funding streams and are designed to cover costs or reinvest into managing tourism resources.

Local governments can explore various mechanisms such as **bed tax, individual attractions such as entry into national parks, or specific user rights such as parking fees**. Mandatory pricing could be complemented by voluntary contributions made by visitors or businesses such as through fundraising events.

(ii)   **Enable smaller-scale options for tourism green finance.** Development partners and financiers can **tailor green finance options to make them accessible to smaller scale** tourism projects, for example by enabling small loans with a straightforward application process or by facilitating clusters of operators to draw down on green financing options. **Developing risk sharing mechanisms can also increase access to finance** by encouraging private investment in sustainable tourism projects. Tourism entrepreneurs can **explore finance through crowdfunding options**; while larger firms like airlines and tour operators can collect and distribute microdonations (Box 15). In tandem, governments and development partners should work to improve the financial literacy of small businesses and MSMEs.

(iii) **Include sustainability criteria in assessing projects for green funding.** Governments should assess standards or formulate new ones to help identify projects or certify their eligibility for green financing (Chapter 5.4). Governments and development partners should consider using sustainability criteria and standards when funding tourism development projects.

(iv)   **Integrate tourism considerations into other initiatives.** Greater financing for sustainable tourism can be achieved by integrating sustainable tourism considerations into other investment projects and programs. National and regional tourism decision-makers should connect with counterparts in other sectors—for example in transport or environmental planning—**to integrate tourism considerations into other sectors** and vice versa. Greater financing for sustainable tourism can be achieved by the more effective integration of sustainable tourism considerations into other investment projects and programs. Investments in transport and livable cities, for example, can be leveraged to meet sustainable tourism goals.

Appendix

Webinars Attended by the Consultants Who Prepared the Study, Susanne Becken and Johanna Loehr

Organizer	Name	Date
ADB and WTO (with UNWTO)	Aid for Trade Stocktaking Event 2021	24/03/2021
Council for Australasian Tourism and Hospitality Education	Destination Management Session	11/02/2021
DRV & GIZ	COVID-19: A Paradigm Shift. Rebuilding A Better Tourism World with Health Security, Diversification, and Free Mobility?	24/09/2020
Eco Tourism Australia	Global Eco Asia-Pacific Tourism Conference	01-03/12/2020
Griffith Asia Institute	Pacific Islands' Tourism during COVID-19: Danger or Opportunity	10/12/2021
Griffith Asia Institute and Pacific Trade Invest Australia	How is Pacific Business Really Doing?	04/03/2021
Institut za Tourizam, The Travel Foundation and Future of Tourism	How Can Tourism Build Back Better? Supporting Recovery and Building Resilience in A Post-Pandemic Landscape	26/03/2021
Japan Tourism Agency, Ministry of Land, Infrastructure, Transport and Tourism and UNWTO Regional Support Office for Asia and the Pacific	Addressing the Critical Need to Tourism Crisis Management: The Significance and Importance of Tourism Crisis Management and How to Respond to Crises	25/02/2021
PATA	PATA Beyond: Travel Recovery Solutions	08-11/02/2021
SPTO	How Can Pacific Tourism SMEs "Bounce Back" Stronger?	25/03/2021
STR	COVID-19 impact on Asia Pacific Hotel Performance	29/01/2021
UNWTO	Quo Vadis Tourism UNWTO Communicating Crisis: Pre, During, Post COVID-19	17/04/2020
World Tourism Network	Tourism & Happiness: for a Brighter Future	19/03/2021

ADB = Asian Development Bank, DRV = Deutscher Reiseverband, GIZ = Deutsche Gesellschaft für Internationale Zusammenarbeit, PATA = Pacific Asia Travel Association, SPTO = South Pacific Tourism Organisation, STR = STR, Inc., UNWTO = United Nations World Tourism Organization.

Source: Authors' compilation.

Expert Interviewees

Expert's Role	Stakeholder Type	Area of Expertise and Work	Location
Tourism Organizations			
CEO	Regional tourism organizations	SIDS, tourism policy, cooperation	Fiji
Senior Sustainability Officer	Regional tourism organizations	SIDS, sustainable tourism	Fiji
Director	UN agency	SDGs, cooperation	Switzerland
CEO	Regional tourism organizations	Interregional collaboration, tourism data, technology, marketing	Thailand
Sustainability Manager	Regional tourism organizations	Community-based tourism, educational tours, sustainability	Thailand
Nontourism Organizations			
Senior Programs Officer	Development organization	Collaboration, economics, SIDS, South Pacific	Australia
Tourism Consultant	Development organization	Collaboration, economics, SIDS, South Pacific	Australia
Policy Analyst	International organization	Policy, economics, indicators	France
Programme Officer	UN agency	Sustainable production and consumption, tourism value chain	France
Project Manager	Technical assistance	Cooperation, sustainable tourism	Germany
Regional Project Manager	NGO	Wildlife (and tourism) expert	Malaysia
Project Director	Technical assistance	Climate change, environmental issues, some tourism	Thailand
Government			
Senior Tourism Officer	Government	Tourism management, policy	Fiji
CEO	Government	Sustainable tourism, tourism marketing, destination management	Kiribati
Tourism Advisor	Intergovernmental organization	Climate change, digital innovation, green recovery	Nepal
Senior Advisor	Government	Pacific cooperation, tourism management	New Zealand
Secretary	Government	Pacific, tourism management, policy	Solomon Islands
Director	Government	Community-based tourism, environmental indicators and standards	Thailand
Director	Government	Sustainable tourism, policy, culture	Vanuatu
Private Sector and Academia			
Cofounder and Director	Consultant	Sustainable tourism, well-being, indicators for tourism	Australia
CEO	Consultant	Tourism development, policies, planning in several Asian countries	Australia

Expert Interviewees *(continued)*

Chairperson, Consultant	Private sector	Lodge owner, tourism consultant, educator	Australia/ Indonesia
CEO	Private sector	Entrepreneur; renewable energy, tourism company	India
Founder, Entrepreneur	Private sector	Ecotourism, community-based tourism, disaster management	India
Lecturer	Expert, academic	Sustainable tourism Indonesia	Indonesia
Professor	Expert, academic	Sustainable tourism, communities, gender	Japan
Managing Director	Consultant	Tourism consultant and GSTC trainer, SDGs, and Agenda 2030	New Zealand
CEO	Consultant	Sustainable tourism, measurement, resource use, business	Singapore

CEO = chief executive officer, SIDS = small island developing states, SDGs = Sustainable Development Goals, GSTC = Global Sustainable Tourism Council, NGO = nongovernment organization, UN = United Nations.

Source: Authors' compilation.

References

M. Abate et al. 2020. Government Support to Airlines in the Aftermath of the COVID-19 Pandemic. *Journal of Air Transport Management*. 89 (101931).

M. M. Aminy. 2020. Can Virtual Tourism Save Local Bsinesses in Tourist Destinations? *The Conversation*. 2 December.

The Asia Foundation. 2021. *Enduring the Pandemic: Rapid Survey in the Impact of COVID-19 on MSMEs in the Tourism Sector and Households in Cambodia*.

Asia-Pacific Economic Cooperation (APEC) 2017. *Developing the Tourism Workforce of the Future in the APEC Region*.

APEC. 2019. SMEs' Integration into Global Value Chains in Services Industries: Tourism Sector.

Asian Development Bank (ADB). 2019. *Improving Education, Skills, and Employment in Tourism—Almaty-Bishkek Economic Corridor*. Manila.

———. 2020. *Asian Development Outlook 2020 Update: Theme Chapter: Wellness in Worrying Times*. Manila.

———. 2020. *Maldives Economic Update 2020*. Manila.

———. Pacific Economic Monitor Series. Manila.

———. 2021. *ADB, EIB Join Forces to Protect Oceans, Support the Blue Economy*. Press release. 15 January.

ADB and Central Asia Regional Economic Cooperation (CAREC). 2018. *Aviation and the role of CAREC. A scoping study*. Manila.

ADB and CAREC. 2021. *Impact of COVID-19 On CAREC Aviation and Tourism*. Manila.

Association of Women for Action and Research. *COVID-19 and the Increase of Domestic Violence against Women: OHCHR Submission by AWARE*.

Australasian British Travel Association. 2021. *Tourism for Good*.

Z. Banhalmi-Zakar et al. 2016. *Mechanisms to Finance Climate Change Adaptation in Australia*. National Climate Change Adaptation Research Facility: Gold Coast.

P. Barkas et al. 2020. International Trade in Travel and Tourism Services: Economic Impact and Policy Responses During the COVID-19 Crisis. *Staff Working Paper*. ERSD-2020-11. Geneva: World Trade Organization.

T. Baum. 2020. COVID-19's Impact on the Hospitality Workforce—New Crisis or Amplification of the Norm? *International Journal of Contemporary Hospitality Management.* 32(9). pp. 2813–2829.

S. Becken. 2014. Water Equity—Contrasting Tourism Water Use with that of the Local Community. *Water Resources and Industry.* 7–8. pp. 9–22.

S. Becken and K. F. Hughey. 2021. Impacts of Changes to Business Travel Practices in Response to the COVID-19 Lockdown in New Zealand. *Journal of Sustainable Tourism.*

S. Becken and B. Mackey. 2017. What Role for Offsetting Aviation Greenhouse Gas Emissions in a Deep-Cut Carbon World? *Journal of Air Transport Management.* 63. pp. 71–83.

S. Becken and P. Pant. 2019. *Airline Initiatives to Reduce Climate Impact. Ways to Accelerate Action.* Madrid: Amadeus.

S. Becken and J. Shuker. 2018. A Framework to Help Destinations Manage Carbon Risk from Aviation Emissions. *Tourism Management.* 71. pp. 294–304.

A. Brooks and V. Heaslip. 2019. Sex Trafficking and Sex Tourism in a Globalised World. *Tourism Review.* 74(5). pp. 1104–1115.

S. Chang et al. 2021. Mobility Network Models of COVID-19 Explain Inequities and Inform Reopening. *Nature.* 589. pp. 82–87.

A. Choi and B. Ritchie. 2014. Willingness to Pay for Flying Carbon Neutral in Australia: An Exploratory Study of Offsetter Profiles. *Journal of Sustainable Tourism.* 22(8). pp. 1236–1256.

J. Coffey et al. 2018. Gender, Sexuality, and Risk in the Practice of Affective Labour for Young Women in Bar Work. *Sociological Research Online.* 23(4). pp. 728–743.

S. Cole. 2012. A Political Ecology of Water Equity and Tourism: A Case Study from Bali. *Annals of Tourism Research.* 39(2). pp. 1221–1241.

The Commonwealth. 2020. *COVID-19 and Tourism: Charting a Sustainable, Resilient Recovery from Small States.*

Destination Thailand News. 2021. *Sustainable Tourism and Those Making it Possible.*

N. Deyshappriya and A.M.D.B. Nawarathna. 2020. Tourism and SME Development: Performance of Tourism SMEs in Coastal Tourist Destinations in Southern Sri Lanka. *ADBI Working Paper Series.* No. 1164. Manila: Asian Development Bank.

L. Dwyer. 2018. Saluting while the Ship Sinks: The Necessity for Tourism Paradigm Change. *Journal of Sustainable Tourism.* 26(1). pp. 29–48.

Earth Changers. 2021. *Sustainable Travel Trends for 2021.*

M. Epler Wood et al. 2019. *Destinations at Risk: The Invisible Burden of Tourism.* The Travel Foundation.

J. Faber et al. 2020. International Aviation and Shipping. In United Nations Environment Programme. 2020. *Emissions Gap Report 2020.* Nairobi.

P. Farrell et al. 2020. COVID-19 and Pacific Food System Resilience: Opportunities to Build a Robust Response. *Food Security*. 12. pp. 783–791.

Forum for the Future. 2020. *From System Shock to System Change: Time to Transform the Future of Sustainability*.

B. P. George and V. Varghese. 2007. Human Rights in Tourism: Conceptualization and Stakeholder Perspectives. *Electronic Journal of Business Ethics and Organization Studies*. 12 (2). pp. 40–48.

M. Ghahremanloo et al. 2021. Impact of the COVID-19 Outbreak on Air Pollution Levels in East Asia. *Science of The Total Environment*. 754 (42226).

Global Policy Journal. 2020. *The Effects of COVID-19 on Migration and Modern Slavery*. Durham.

Global Sustainable Tourism Council (GSTC). 2016. *GSTC Industry Criteria—Suggested Performance Indicators for Hotels and Accommodations*.

R. Golden Kroner et al. 2021. COVID-Era Policies and Economic Recovery Plans: Are Governments Building Back Better for Protected and Conserved Areas? *PARKS*. 27. pp. 135–148.

H. Goodwin. 2012. Ten Years of Responsible Tourism: *An Assessment in Progress in Responsible Tourism 2(1)*. Oxford: Goodfellow.

Government of Australia, Queensland Tourism Industry Council. 2018. *Building a Resilient Tourism Industry: Queensland Tourism Climate Change Response Plan*. Brisbane.

Government of India, Ministry of Electronics and Information Technology. 2020. *Dekho Apna Desh*.

Government of New Zealand, Parliamentary Commissioner for the Environment. 2021. *Not 100%—But Four Steps Closer to Sustainable Tourism*.

Government of Thailand, Ministry of Tourism and Sports. 2020. *Tourism Statistics*.

Government of Thailand, Ministry of Tourism and Sports, Tourism Authority of Thailand. 2019. *The Development of Tourism Connectivity (in Thai)*. Bangkok.

Government of Thailand, Ministry of Tourism and Sports, Tourism Authority of Thailand. 2020. *TAT Highlights Travel Promotions for Expats in Thailand*. Bangkok.

Government of Thailand, Ministry of Higher Education, Science, Research and Innovation. 2021. *BCG Strategies (in Thai)*.

Government of Vanuatu, Department of Tourism. 2020. *Phase 1: Response. Immediate Safety, Response and Economic Recovery Effort*.

Government of Vanuatu, Department of Tourism Vanuatu. 2021. *Vanuatu Sustainable Tourism Strategy 2021–2025*.

Greater Mekong Subregion Secretariat. 2020. *Myanmar Releases Strategic Roadmap for Tourism Recovery*.

U. Gretzel et al. 2020. E-Tourism beyond COVID-19: A Call for Transformative Research. *Information Technology and Tourism*. 22. pp. 187–203.

Griffith University. 2014. *From Challenges to Solutions. 2nd White Paper on Tourism and Water: Providing the Business Case.*

C. M. Hall. 2007. Tourism, Governance and the (Mis-)location of Power. In *Tourism, Power and Space.* London: Routledge. pp. 247–269.

C. Hepburn et al. 2020. Will COVID-19 Fiscal Recovery Packages Accelerate or Retard Progress on Climate Change? *Oxford Review of Economic Policy.* 36(Supplement_1). pp. S359–S381.

J. Higham et al. 2016. Climate Change, Tourist Air Travel and Radical Emissions Reduction. *Journal of Cleaner Production.* 111. pp. 336–347.

S. Hiltner and L. Fisher. 2021. How Bad Was 2020 for Tourism? Look at the Numbers. *The New York Times.* 27 July.

E. Hunt. 2021. Charge More for Flights to Deter Tourists and Help the Planet, Says Air New Zealand Adviser. *The Guardian.*

International Air Transport Association. 2020. *Air Passenger Market Analysis.*

International Civil Aviation Organization (ICAO). 2021. *Effects of Novel Coronavirus (COVID-19) on Civil Aviation: Economic Impact Analysis.*

International Labour Organization (ILO). 2020. *COVID-19 and Employment in the Tourism Sector: Impact and Response in Asia and the Pacific.*

ILO. 2020. *ILO Monitor: COVID-19 and the World of Work, Third Edition.*

International Monetary Fund (IMF). 2020. *Samoa: Request for Disbursement Under the Rapid Credit Facility-Press Release; Staff Report; and Statement by the Executive Director for Samoa.*

IMF. 2021. *Policy Responses to COVID-19.*

H. Janta et al. 2011. Employment Experiences of Polish Migrant Workers in the UK Hospitality Sector. *Tourism Management.* 32(5). pp. 1006–1019.

Journal of Hospitality and Tourism Research. *Exploring the Multiple Benefits of Ecosystem-Based Adaptation in Tourism for Climate Risks and Destination Well-Being.*

C. P. Keller. 1987. Stages of Peripheral Tourism Development—Canada's Northwest Territories. *Tourism Management.* 8(1). pp. 20–32.

D. Koh. 2020. Migrant Workers and COVID-19. *Occupational and Environmental Medicine.* 77(9). pp. 634–636.

A. Lasso and H. Dahles. 2018. Are Tourism Livelihoods Sustainable? Tourism Development and Economic Transformation on Komodo Island, Indonesia. *Asia Pacific Journal of Tourism Research.* 23(5). pp. 473–485.

C. Le Quéré et al. 2020. Temporary Reduction in Daily Global CO2 Emissions during the COVID-19 Forced Confinement. *Nature Climate Change.* 10(7). pp. 647–653.

D. S. Lee et al. 2020. The Contribution of Global Aviation to Anthropogenic Climate Forcing for 2000 to 2018. *Atmospheric Environment.* 244 (117834).

M. Lenzen et al. 2018. The Carbon Footprint of Global Tourism. *Nature Climate Change*. 8. pp. 522–528.

P. Lindsey et al. 2020. Conserving Africa's Wildlife and Wildlands through the COVID-19 Crisis and Beyond. *Nature Ecology and Evolution*. 4. pp. 1300–1310.

The Mainichi. 2018. *About 90% of the Marine Plastic Waste Originates in 10 Rivers in Asia and Africa: Study*.

A. Mahmood et al. 2020. COVID-19 and Frequent Use of Hand Sanitizers; Human Health and Environmental Hazards by Exposure Pathways. *Science of the Total Environment*. 742 (140561).

A. Matheison and G. Wall. 1982. *Tourism: Economic, Physical and Social Impacts*. New York: Longman.

McKinsey & Company. 2020. *COVID-19 and Gender Equality: Countering the Regressive Effects*.

McKinsey & Company. 2020. *Reimagining the $9 Trillion Tourism Economy—What Will It Take?*

Mekong Tourism. Lao PDR: *New Project to Protect Landscapes and Enhance Livelihoods*.

X. Meng et al. 2013. A CGE Assessment of Singapore's Tourism Policies. *Tourism Management*. 34. pp. 25–36.

MFAT and SPTO. 2020. *Pacific Tourism: Covid 19 Impact and Recovery. Sector Status Report: Phase 1B*.

E. Mossberg. 2021. Host Communities Are at the Core of Tomorrow's Sustainable Tourism. *The Good Tourism Blog*.

A. Movono. 2017. Conceptualising Destinations as a Vanua: An Examination of the Evolution and Resilience of a Fijian Social and Ecological System. In J. Cheer and A. Lew, eds. *Understanding Tourism Resilience: Adapting to Environmental Change*. London: Routledge.

A. Movono et al. 2018. Fijian Culture and the Environment: A Focus on the Ecological and Social Interconnectedness of Tourism Development. *Journal of Sustainable Tourism*. 26(3). pp. 451–469.

A. Movono and R. Scheyvens. 2020. Pacific Tourism is Desperate for a Waccine and Travel Freedoms, But the Industry Must Learn from This Crisis. *The Conversation*. 25 November.

A. Neef 2019. *Tourism, Land Grabs and Displacement: A Study with Particular Focus on the Global South*. Auckland: Auckland University.

Office of National Higher Education Science Research and Innovation Policy Council. 2021. BCG in Action.

T. I. Oktavianti. 2020. Jakarta Records Spike in Domestic Violence Reports During Work-From-Home Period. *The Jakarta Post*. 7 April.

Organisation for Economic Co-operation and Development (OECD). 2016. *Entrepreneurship at a Glance 2016*. Paris: OECD Publishing.

OECD. 2020. *COVID-19 and the Aviation Industry: Impact and Policy Responses*.

OECD. 2021. Managing Tourism Development for Sustainable and Inclusive Recovery. *OECD Tourism Papers*. 2021/01. Paris: OECD Publishing.

K. Pasanchay and C. Schott. 2021. *Community-Based Tourism Homestays' Capacity to Advance the Sustainable Development Goals: A Holistic Sustainable Livelihood Perspective. Tourism Management Perspectives.* 37.

Pacific Asia Travel Association (PATA). 2020. *COVID-19 and The Tourism Sector: A Comparison of Policy Response in Asia Pacific.*

T. D. Pham. 2019. Tourism Productivity Theory and Measurement for Policy Implications: The Case of Australia. *Journal of Travel Research.*

T. D. Pham et al. 2020. Visa Policies and Tourist Mobility of Asian Markets: Key Challenges and Determinants. *Tourism Management Perspectives.* Unpublished.

P. Phromkade. 2020. *Reaching Malaysia's Women Migrant Workers amid COVID-19 Crisis.* Brussels: European Commission.

J. Quintuña and D. Marcelo. 2020. *Estimated Impact of COVID-19 on Water Needs and Volume and Quality of Wastewater.*

Y. Ram. 2018. Hostility or Hospitality? A Review on Violence, Bullying and Sexual Harassment in the Tourism and Hospitality Industry. *Current Issues in Tourism.* 21(7). pp. 760–774.

J. Rockström et al. 2009. A Safe Operating Space for Humanity. *Nature.* 461(7263). pp. 472–475.

P. F. Rupani et al. 2020. Coronavirus Pandemic (COVID-19) and Its Natural Environmental Impacts. *International Journal of Environmental Science and Technology.* 2020 (1). pp. 1–12.

A. Rylance and A. Spenceley. 2017. Reducing Economic Leakages from Tourism: A Value Chain Assessment of the Tourism Industry in Kasane, Botswana. *Development Southern Africa.* 34(3). pp. 295–313.

R. Scheyvens, and A. Movono. 2020. *Development in a World of Disorder: Tourism, COVID-19 and the Adaptivity of South Pacific People.* Palmerston North, NZ: Massey University, Institute of Development Studies.

D. Scott. 2008. *Climate Change and Tourism: Responding to Global Challenges.* Madrid: United Nations World Tourism Organization and Paris: United Nations Environment Programme.

D. Scott et al. 2019. A Global Climate Change Vulnerability Index for the Tourism Sector. *Annals of Tourism Research.* 77. pp. 49–61.

E. Shamshiry et al. 2011. Integrated Models for Solid Waste Management in Tourism Regions: Langkawi Island, Malaysia. *Journal of Environmental and Public Health.* 709549. pp. 1–5.

I. Scoones, 2009. Livelihoods Perspectives and Rural Development. *The Journal of Peasant Studies.* 36(1). Pp.171–196.

R. Sharpley. 2020. Tourism, Sustainable Development and the Theoretical Divide: 20 Years On. *Journal of Sustainable Tourism.* 11. pp. 1932–1946.

Skift. 2018. *Where Luxury is Going Next.*

Skift. 2020. *Asia Tourism Tackles Climate Change: It Gets Confusing.*

R. Sleeman and D. G. Simmons. 2004. *Tourism Planning Toolkit for Local Government*. Lincoln: Tourism Recreation Research and Education Centre, Lincoln University.

M. Soshkin. 2019. *If You Build It, They Will Come: Why Infrastructure Is Crucial to Tourism Growth and Competitiveness*.

A. Sourvinou and V. Filimonau. 2018. Planning for an Environmental Management Programme in a Luxury Hotel and Its Perceived Impact on Staff: An Exploratory Case Study. *Journal of Sustainable Tourism*. 26(4). pp. 649–667.

STR. 2021. *COVID-19 Impact on Asia Pacific Hotel Performance*.

A. Taub. 2020. A New Covid-19 Crisis: Domestic Abuse Rises Worldwide. *The New York Times*.

G. Topham. 2021. UK Set to Cut Air Passenger Duty on Domestic Flights. *The Guardian*. 10 March.

Travalyst. 2021. *The Re-emergence of Travel: A Travalyst View*.

A. Trupp and S. Sunanta. 2017. Gendered Practices in Urban Ethnic Tourism in Thailand. *Annals of Tourism Research*. 64. pp. 76–86.

L. Twining Ward and J. F. McComb. 2020. *COVID-19 and Tourism in South Asia: Opportunities for Sustainable Regional Outcomes*. Washington, DC: World Bank.

United Nations (UN). 2020. *Policy Brief: COVID-19 and Transforming Tourism*. New York.

UN. 2020. *Sustainable Development Knowledge Platform—Voluntary National Reviews Database*.

UN Conference on Trade and Development. 2020. *COVID-19 Requires Gender-Equal Responses to Save Economies*.

United Nations Economic and Social Commission for Asia and the Pacific. 2019. *Tourism Satellite Account for India (TSAI)*. Bangkok.

United Nations Educational, Scientific and Cultural Organization (UNESCO). 2018. Safeguarding World Heritage: UNESCO Asia-Pacific In Graphic Detail #6.

UNESCO. 2020. *Monitoring World Heritage Site Closures*.

UNEP. 2021. *Are We Building Back Better? Evidence from 2020 and Pathways for Inclusive Green Recovery Spending*.

UN Myanmar. 2020. *Making Migration Safe and Fair for Women Workers*.

United Nations World Tourism Organization (UNWTO). 2015. *Affiliate Members Global Reports, Volume eleven— Public-Private Partnerships: Tourism Development*. Madrid.

———. 2019. *Global Report on Women in Tourism - Second Edition*. Madrid.

———. 2020. *COVID—19 Related Travel Restrictions a Global Review for Tourism*. Madrid.

———. 2020. *International Tourism and COVID—19*. Dashboard.

———. 2021. *COVID-19: Measures to Support Travel and Tourism*.

———. 2021. *World Tourism Barometer*. Madrid.

———. 2021. *UNWTO Inclusive Recovery Guide—Sociocultural Impacts of Covid-19, Issue 3: Women in Tourism.* Madrid.

UNWTO and UNEP. 2017. *Tourism and the Sustainable Development Goals—Journey to 2030*. Madrid.

M. Velasco. 2016. Tourism Policy. In A. Farazmand, ed., *Global Encyclopedia of Public Administration, Public Policy, and Governance*. Cham: Springer.

P. Vendergeest et al. 2021. Migrant Worker Segregation Doesn't Work: COVID-19 Lessons from Southeast Asia. *The Conversation*.

S. Vunibola and I. Leweniqila. 2020. Food Security in Covid19: Insights from Indigenous Fijian Communities. *Oceania*. 1. pp. 81–88.

J. Waithaka et al. 2021. Impacts of COVID-19 on Protected and Conserved Areas: A Global Overview and Regional Perspectives. *Parks*. 27. pp. 41–56.

J. C. Wang and K. Huang. 2013. Energy Consumption Characteristics of Hotel's Marketing Preference for Guests from Regions Perspectives. *Energy*. 52. pp. 173–84.

C. Warren and S. Becken. 2016. Saving Energy and Water in Tourist Accommodation: A Systematic Literature Review. *International Journal of Hospitality Management*. 19(3). pp. 289–303.

C. Warren et al. 2016. Using Persuasive Communication to Co-create Behavioural Change—Engaging with Guests to Save Resources at Tourist Accommodation Facilities. *Journal of Sustainable Tourism*. 25(7). pp. 935–954.

C. Warren et al. 2018. Transitioning to Smart Sustainable Tourist Accommodation: Service Innovation Results. *Journal of Cleaner Production*. 201. pp. 599–608.

J. Wisansing and T. Berno. 2019. *Master Plan ASEAN Gastronomy*. Ministry of Tourism and Sports. Bangkok.

N. Wongsamuth. 2021. *Migrant Workers Suffer as Coronavirus Causes Surge in Thailand*. Reuters. 8 January 2021.

Workplace Gender Equality Agency. 2020. *Gendered Impact of COVID-19*.

World Commission on Environment and Development. 1987. *Our Common Future*. New York: United Nations.

World Economic Forum (WEF). 2017. *Healthy Coral Reefs Are Good For Tourism – and Tourism Can Be Good for Reefs*.

WEF. 2019. *The Travel and Tourism Competitiveness Report 2019*. Geneva.

World Resources Institute. 2019. *Aqueduct Water Risk Atlas*.

World Travel and Tourism Council (WTTC). 2019. *Seamless Traveller Journey Emerging Models Overview and Findings Report*.

WTTC. 2020. *Economic Impacts Reports*.

WTTC. 2020. *To Recovery and Beyond: The Future of Travel and Tourism in the Wake of COVID-19.*

World Wide Fund for Nature (WWF). 2018. *Tourists Cause Almost 40% Spike in Plastic Entering the Mediterranean Sea Each Summer.*

WWF. 2020. *The Loss of Nature and the Rise of Pandemics. Protecting Human and Planetary Health.*

Y. Yang et al. 2020. Monitoring the Global COVID-19 Impact on Tourism: The COVID19 Tourism Index. *Annals of Tourism Research.* 103120.